ELITE PERFORMANCE

# Running

## FROM MIDDLE DISTANCE TO MARATHON

ELITE PERFORMANCE

# Running

## FROM MIDDLE DISTANCE
## TO MARATHON

### Dr Garry Palmer and Alex Reid

A & C BLACK • LONDON

For my Dad, who is always in my thoughts, from Garry.
For my sister, Naomi, who is a continuous inspiration to me, and for Malc and our daughter, Isla, who makes us complete, from Alex.

Published by A&C Black Publishers Ltd
36 Soho Square, London W1D 3QY
www.acblack.com

First edition 2009

ISBN 978 14081 1215 1

A CIP catalogue record for this book is available from the British Library.

**Acknowledgements**
Cover photograph © istockphoto
Inside photographs © istock ii, 6, 40, 102, 130, 170; © Garry Palmer 33; © Grant Pritchard 43–45, 46, 47, 48, 65, 66, 81, 82, 83, 85, 86, 105–107, 112–114, 116, 161; © Ian Walton/Getty Images 1; © PA Photos 175, 178a; © scienceinsport.com 154, 178b
Illustrations by Mark Silver (46, 67, 68, 70, 82, 88, 89, 147), Jeff Edwards (9, 11, 12, 13, 15, 20, 23, 24, 166), Tina Howe/Mark Silver (138) and Garry Palmer (25, 34, 38, 39)
Designed by James Watson
Commissioned by Charlotte Atyeo
Edited by Kate Burkhalter

This book is produced using paper that is made from wood grown in managed, sustainable forests. It is natural, renewable and recyclable. The logging and manufacturing processes conform to the environmental regulations of the country of origin.

Typeset in MetaPlusNormal by Palimpsest Book Production Limited, Grangemouth, Stirlingshire.

Printed and bound in China by Printing Co., Ltd.

# CONTENTS

*Acknowledgements*                                             viii
*Foreword by Liz Yelling*                                         1
*Foreword by John Bryant*                                        2
*Preface*                                                        3

## PART ONE: PHYSIOLOGY AND TRAINING
**1  Physiology of running**                                     8
  Oxygen is the key                                    8
  Circulatory changes                                  9
  Energy production                                    11
  $VO_2$max: a determinant of performance              12
  It's not just about oxygen                           13
**2  Principles of training**                                    16
  So, you want to go faster?                           16
  The building blocks of training                      17
  Choosing your event                                  20
  Determinants of performance                          21
  The five key elements of training                    22
  The overload principle                               23
  Basic periodisation                                  24
  Training with heart rate                             26
  Risks of exercising                                  27
  Self-administered treadmill test                     28
  Field testing                                        29
  The benefits of physiological testing                33
  What the numbers mean                                34
  The training zones                                   35
  Training effectively                                 38

## PART TWO: INJURY PREVENTION
**3  Flexibility and stretching: concepts and rationale**        42
  The benefits of stretching                           42

Static stretching                                               **43**
Dynamic flexibility                                             **44**
PNF technique                                                   **45**
Myofascial release                                             **46**
Factors limiting flexibility                                   **47**
Stretching plan: practical application                         **48**
4  **Over-training, injury prevention and performance**        **50**
Evaluation of progress                                         **50**
Over-training: immune system response to exercise              **52**
How to avoid over-training                                     **54**
Symptoms of over-training                                      **55**
Using resting heart rate to identify over-training             **56**
5  **Running injuries**                                        **63**
Screening                                                      **63**
Common running injuries                                        **64**
Foot care                                                      **71**
PRICE                                                          **75**
Ice or heat?                                                   **76**
Rehabilitation of your injury: practical guidelines            **78**
Core function                                                  **88**
6  **Rest and recovery**                                       **92**
Recovery techniques                                            **92**
Rest days                                                      **95**
Application of recovery principles                             **96**

**PART THREE: TRAINING DRILLS AND PROGRAMMES**
7  **Functional drills and sessions**                          **104**
Running drills, speed and agility                              **104**
Strength training                                              **107**
Strength training: research for runners                        **110**
Exercise selection                                             **112**
Plyometrics, resisted running and hill training                **115**
8  **Training programme design**                               **120**
Putting it all into practice: exercise prescription            **120**
Building your training programme                               **121**
Adapting the training programmes for other distances           **129**

## PART FOUR: NUTRITION

9  **General nutrition**    **132**
   Basic dietary needs    **132**
   Water balance    **136**
   Resting dietary composition    **137**
   Normal, 'healthy' diet    **138**
10 **Fuel for sport**    **139**
   Energy efficiency    **139**
   Effect of diet    **141**
   Repeated-days training    **142**
   Protein burning    **143**
   The importance of hydration    **143**
11 **Optimal nutrition for exercise**    **145**
   Nutrition for recovery    **145**
   Nutrition prior to training    **148**
   Nutrition during training    **150**
   Nutrition for training camps    **154**
   Race-day nutrition    **155**
   Putting it all into practice    **158**
12 **Nutritional targets**    **160**
   Assessing your needs    **160**
   Assessing body composition    **160**
   Keeping a diet diary    **163**
   Calculating your needs    **164**
   Weight loss: a balancing act    **166**
   Energy balance    **168**

## PART FIVE: RACE DAY

13 **Putting it all together**    **172**
   What to take with you    **172**
   The day before    **174**
   Race-day nutrition strategies    **175**
   Race tactics    **175**
   It's all in the mind . . .    **177**
   It's all over: how to recover    **178**

*Useful websites*    **180**
*References*    **181**
*Index*    **183**

# FOREWORD

*John Bryant has a wealth of experience as an athlete and coach. He has also served as editor of various newspapers, including the* Daily Telegraph, *the* Times *and the* Daily Mail. *He is the author of* The London Marathon – History of the Greatest Race on Earth *and* The Marathon Makers *and is currently Chairman of the Press Association Trust.*

Writing as a runner with almost half a century of experience, it is a long and sometimes haphazard process to build up a body of evidence and tips on which to base your training. You pick up a hint here from a running magazine, you learn a training technique there from a training partner, you pick up what champions do and what scientists write about.

Sometimes this training lore is good, but among the rag-bag that athletes pick up is a wealth of varying information, much of which has been overtaken by time, some half-remembered and some simply not backed up by the evidence.

*Elite Performance Running: From Middle Distance to Marathon* does exactly what it promises on the cover. It is both encyclopaedic in its approach and bang up-to-date. It will remind veteran runners of half-forgotten training principles. And it will give new runners an invaluable guide that should stop them making many of the mistakes which could shorten, impair, or even end a career in running.

The authors are both experts in their field. Dr Garry Palmer is a sports scientist with vast experience of working with athletes in a wide variety of sports to World Championship and Olympic level. As an athlete he was a county-level runner, representing Hampshire. As a triathlete he represented Great Britain at World Age Group Championships.

Alex Reid has competed internationally, representing England at Basketball and has won 21 International Caps. She became the Head Strength & Conditioning Coach for Fulham Football Club, and more recently, she has worked for Tottenham Hotspur Football Club where she managed all the strength, conditioning and rehabilitation of the professional players.

Their book aims to provide readers with a comprehensive and up-to-date scientific approach to physiology, training and nutrition, presented at a level understandable to enthusiasts, athletes and coaches alike.

From personal experience, having run in 26 London Marathons (so far!), I also know that it will prove a wise guide to all those novices or charity runners looking to take up running for the first time. It will give them valuable advice on the dangers of over-training; good sense on everything from what to eat and how fast to run; and, more importantly, tips on how to enjoy every footstep of their running.

# PREFACE
ALEX REID

Running is an obvious way to keep in shape and, indeed, is an activity that hundreds of thousands of people take part in every day.

Some run to keep fit, some run for the social interaction with other people, some run for charity, for a new year's resolution, for weight loss. Some run to reduce stress and increase well-being, some do it because they feel they should! But one thing is certain: although running is a simple enough activity that can be done just about anywhere in the world, to run optimally, injury-free and with purpose takes more than just pounding the roads.

Every year, thousands of people compete in marathons all over the world. The high-profile events, like those in London, Chicago and New York, attract thousands of entries and participants; 35,694 people finished the London Marathon in 2007, making it the largest ever. It is estimated finishers have raised more than £360 million in sponsorship for numerous charities over the years; a record-breaking £46.5 million was raised for good causes by the 2007 event alone, making the London Marathon a Guinness world record holder as the largest single annual fundraising event in the world (for more information, see www.london-marathon.co.uk).

In addition, thousands of people will participate in 10 km events and fun runs, as well as more competitive events. This sounds great in principle, but many of these participants will be in need of some guidance and knowledge to help them achieve their goals.

Many will experience injury along the way or will fail to prepare optimally, purely because they have not been privy to the right knowledge to help them on their way. The entry forms are in. Your place has been accepted, now what?! Well, the information is readily available – it is all here.

This book offers a way to acquire some research-based, in-depth information regarding how you will go through your journey in order to reach your destination – safe and sound.

Every year in about October/November time I receive emails from friends, family and colleagues, who announce 'Next year, I am running the London Marathon – please sponsor me for this great cause.' They are often first-timers, who may or may not have been active before.

It is always a great cause, and a noble effort by the individuals who are driven to achieve, and raise millions for charities all over the world. The question is, though, how can they do it? How can they achieve this tremendous goal and run 26 miles 385 yards as well as they can, or even complete a 10 km event?

Of course, it can be done by grit and determination alone – even if you walk round to get your medal and collect your sponsorship money – but technology is changing, sports science is now accessible to the fun runners as well as the elite athletes, so why not sit down and take advantage of that science and make your journey a bit more calculated, a bit more prescribed, a lot safer, with an increased opportunity for success as a result of this knowledge?

My husband and I went along to watch a friend run the 2008 Flora London Marathon. It was the first time I had been to such an event. It was amazing and inspirational, and our friend finished with great pride, raising much-needed money for his chosen charity, which is very close to his heart. It was fantastic!

It gave me the desire to get my running shoes on and do it myself in 2009. I think this is how many people feel when they watch an inspirational event like the London Marathon. I also felt inspired when my sister and her husband ran the Windsor Half Marathon; they built up to it over a few months, completing a few 10 km runs along the way.

I remember my husband telling me that Brian, his colleague who had finished the London Marathon, couldn't walk properly for a week afterwards! Wow, that's tough, but under-standable bearing in mind the challenge and what Brian had achieved. However, maybe if Brian had been aware of some relatively simple sports science principles, he could have recovered better, even been better prepared to help him on his journey. He still

finished, and in good time, and he raised a lot of money, but could it have been easier for him, mentally and physically? With a copy of *Elite Performance: Running*, it may well have been.

This book is aimed at those who want to succeed, from 10 km through to the marathon. It is a practical 'how to' guide, which aims to provide an insight into the modern, research-based sports science principles that will increase your understanding of how to reach your personal targets and running-based goals.

The book addresses all concepts of applied sports science: simple things like why you should use ice instead of heat on an acute injury, and not have a hot bath after an intense session; what to eat and drink and when; what actually happens to your body when you exercise, and how to train to optimise this; as well as over-training issues and risks. It also addresses recovery and injury potential, foot care and what to do if you get injured, including rehabilitation guidelines to ensure you get back on track as safely and promptly as possible.

In addition, a number of drills, and strength and conditioning exercises are included, which will enhance your running programme. Gone are the days when you 'just run' to keep in great shape; now you can complement your running programme with a number of drills and exercises that will lead to an even stronger performance on race day.

This is a resource to which every runner – whether novice, first-time participant, or long-timer who wants to learn more about the body and how best to train – should have access. It will guide you through the challenges along the way and provide a practical insight that is no longer exclusive to the elite performer.

The information you need is all here, so good luck and 'Go for it!'

# 1

# PHYSIOLOGY AND TRAINING

# 1

# PHYSIOLOGY OF RUNNING

Running is simple, right? One foot in front of the other and off you go. As babies we learn to crawl, then we learn to walk, then we run. Nearly everyone can do it. Our motivation for running may be for the enjoyment and personal challenge, to aid fitness, to gain or lose weight, or to raise money for charity. Whatever the motivation, the goal of most runners is to do their best.

So, how can you go faster? Why can't you run as fast as the elite athletes? How can you train to run more effectively? What is holding your performance back? Having a basic knowledge of the physiology of running will help answer these questions.

The physiology (the science of the function of a living organism, which includes the mechanical, physical and biochemical aspects of organs, and the cells of which it is made) of the human body is a vast and often complex subject. The changes in physiological responses that occur when exercising can make the study of running quite complex. However, these changes also provide insight into what is needed to ultimately improve performance.

## Oxygen is the key

The main physiological limitation to the ability to run is oxygen consumption. All living organisms need oxygen to survive. During exercise the need for oxygen increases. This is simply because additional oxygen is needed at the working muscle to assist in the metabolism of fuel, which in turn provides the energy for muscular contraction. So, in order to run, an increased amount of oxygen needs to be delivered to the relevant muscle groups.

The air around us (which contains approximately 21 per cent oxygen) is drawn into the lungs by the contraction of the diaphragm and intercostals (the muscles between the ribs). A pressure difference causes the oxygen to then diffuse across the wall of the lung (moving from high to low concentration levels) and combines with haemoglobin in the blood. The freshly oxygenated blood is first taken back to the heart, before being pumped to supply all parts of the body. Once the blood reaches the muscle, the oxygen diffuses into the muscle (*see* Figure 1.1). This oxygen is then used for the aerobic (oxygen-using) metabolic processes within the muscle to produce the energy for muscular contraction.

The aerobic metabolism produces the waste product, carbon dioxide ($CO_2$). The $CO_2$ diffuses back into the blood from the muscle. It is then transported back via the circulatory system to the lung, where, again, the process of diffusion is used to expel the $CO_2$ via the breath.

While increased oxygen is needed to supply energy for muscular activity, the regulation of the breathing response is an involuntary process that is controlled by the respiratory centre in the brain. Surprisingly, the body is more sensitive to $CO_2$ levels than to the oxygen demands of the body. If $CO_2$ levels in the blood increase, as they will at the onset of exercise, the increased $CO_2$ concentration in the blood will trigger the movements of inspiration. In turn, more air is drawn into the lungs, more oxygen is taken into the blood, and thus more oxygen becomes available for supply to the muscle.

## Circulatory changes

Increased ventilation alone will not give rise to increased oxygen delivery to the working muscle. In order for that to occur, there needs to be an increase in cardiac output. Cardiac output is the measure of what is needed from the circulatory system to meet the demands of physical activity. It is determined by the product of stroke volume (the amount of blood pumped with each beat of the heart) and heart rate:

cardiac output = stroke volume x heart rate

### CARDIAC OUTPUT AND STROKE VOLUME

*Cardiac output* is the volume of blood pumped by the heart per minute (ml/blood/min). It is a function of heart rate and stroke volume. The *heart rate* is simply the number of heart-beats per minute. The *stroke volume* is the volume of blood, in millilitres (ml), pumped out of the heart with each beat. Increasing either heart rate or stroke volume increases cardiac output.

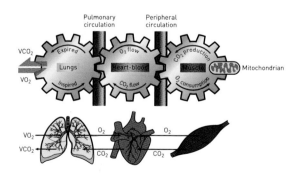

**Figure 1.1 Schematic of oxygen kinetics**

Therefore, in order to be able to supply more oxygenated blood to the working muscle, stroke volume and/or heart rate must increase.

For untrained individuals there is only a small increase in stroke volume from rest to exercise, whereas for trained individuals this increase is more marked. However, in both cases the biggest change in stroke volume occurs between rest and moderate exercise, and stroke volume will be at its highest before most individuals reach 40 or 50 per cent of their maximum rate of oxygen uptake. Beyond these levels, further increases in cardiac output can be achieved only by an increase in heart rate. This is primarily the reason that many athletes will use a heart rate monitor to determine exercise intensity during training (a topic that is examined in more depth in chapter 2).

The drive for increases in cardiac output, and therefore heart rate, during exercise can, as in the case of the ventilator drivers, be traced to the working muscle. At the onset of exercise, neural (nerve), chemical and hormonal changes will cause the distribution of blood flow within the body to be automatically regulated. Specifically, blood flow changes as a direct response to the chemical environment of the local muscle tissue.

At rest under normal conditions, the liver and kidneys receive almost half the circulating blood, while the skeletal muscles receive only about 15 per cent of it. During intense exercise, blood is directed to the areas where it is needed most, with as much as 80 per cent of the available blood going to the muscle. The biggest stimulus to the direction of blood flow appears to be oxygen demand by the muscle. As the oxygen use in the muscle rises, oxygen availability drops. Local arterioles (small arteries that carry blood to capillaries) dilate to allow greater blood flow to the particular area with most demand, and therefore increase the oxygen supply. Changes in concentration of other nutrients, and increases in metabolic by-products or inflammatory chemicals can also influence blood supply to bring in required substances or clear potentially harmful ones.

In addition to this local control of blood flow to the tissue, the body uses the sympathetic nervous system to control the flow of blood around the whole body. Subconscious control of nerves within the blood vessel walls allows for constriction of the arterioles. This 'vasoconstriction' will cause a reduction in blood flow to areas of the body where oxygenated blood is not in such great demand, allowing it to be directed towards the areas where it is needed most, without large fluctuations in blood pressure, which would have a negative impact on the body. In this way the working muscle will receive a constant and appropriate supply of oxygen to best meet the metabolic demand of the activity that is taking place.

This overview of the ventilator and circulatory responses of the cardiovascular system during exercise is highly simplified. Yet it serves to indicate just a few of the complex interactions that take place within the body during exercise. What must be remembered is that the key driving force in the ability for the muscle to perform endurance activity is sufficient supplies of oxygen. Without the presence of oxygen, this activity cannot be sustained.

## Energy production

Ventilation and circulation work in combination in response to the demand for oxygen from the working muscle to, in turn, meet the demand for energy production in endurance exercise. However, the delivery of oxygen to the working muscle is not the only factor in the production of energy.

Energy in the cell is not stored in the same form as the food source from which it was obtained. Rather, it is 'harvested' from the fuel sources into the high-energy compound adenosine triphosphate (ATP). The potential energy within ATP is used to provide the energy for *all* the cell's energy-requiring processes. It is the breakdown of ATP to adenosine diphosphate (ADP) and a single phosphate (p) that produces energy:

$$ATP \leftrightarrow ADP + P + Energy$$

However, the stored ATP available in the muscle is only sufficient to provide energy for muscular contraction for a second or two at most (*see* Figure 1.2).

To provide energy for maximal bouts of strength or power, peaking at about six seconds'

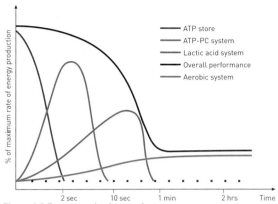
**Figure 1.2 Energy production continuum**

duration, another compound, creatine phosphate (CP) is used to produce more ATP (ATP-CP in Figure 1.2). As the availability of creatine phosphate is also limited, beyond this time ATP needs to be yielded by biochemically breaking down the available energy from carbohydrate.

The process of breaking down glycogen (the storage form of carbohydrate) is called glycolysis. In the first part of the glycolytic pathway, two molecules of ATP are yielded and pyruvate is formed. As the process needs to be rapid, it takes place without the presence of oxygen and is therefore oxygen independent. However, as this is the system used during high-intensity exercise when oxygen uptake is often inadequate, it is often referred to, perhaps incorrectly, as anaerobic glycolysis (as the mechanism would still be used to provide ATP rapidly, without the use of oxygen, even if high amounts of oxygen were available).

When the rate of pyruvate formation is too great for the amount of oxygen available to allow it to

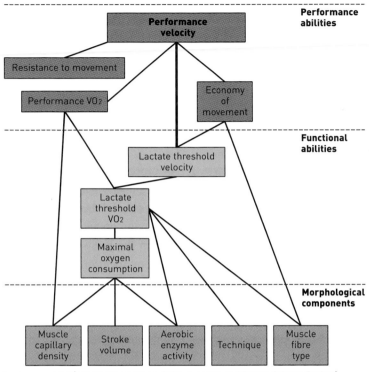

**Figure 1.4 Endurance performance model (adapted from Coyle, 1995, Exercise and Sports Science Review)**

who requires less oxygen to run at a given pace, and therefore uses less energy to do so. Further morphological components will impact the individual's $VO_2$max, LT or economy of movement.

In his review, Coyle went on to validate his model for a group of endurance cyclists and found that, when cycling for 40 km, performance velocity was predicted with 94 per cent of variance being accounted for when LT power (measured as LT velocity in runners) and muscle capillary density were considered. Coyle's validation has not been undertaken specifically for runners to date, but he suggested that the model would be appropriate for all endurance performance.

However, a review published by Sjodin and Svedenhag (1985) suggests that, despite having similar performance capabilities, there appear to be large differences in $VO_2$max measurements in marathon runners. They suggest that the complementary factors of $VO_2$max, oxygen uptake at a running speed of 15 km/h (running economy) and the percentage of $VO_2$max at marathon pace all account for the individual performance of the marathon runner. In contrast to Coyle, however, they suggest that these variables also explain differences in 'anaerobic threshold'.

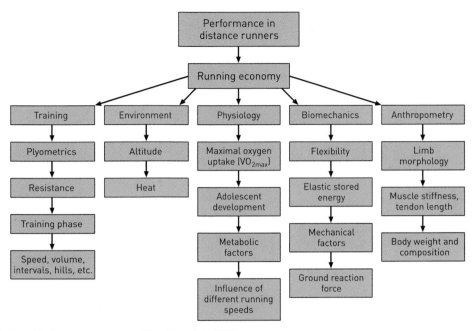

**Figure 1.5 Factors affecting running economy (Saunders et al., 2004)**

## Running economy

More recently, in 2007, Professors Foster and Lucia, in their conference paper entitled 'Running economy: the forgotten factor in elite perform-ance', concluded that 'Since high level athletes already have, either through training or selection, high values for $VO_2$max and the ability to sustain $VO_2$max, it may be that future improvement in running performance will depend on improved economy.'

This may actually be considerably more complex than it sounds. For as complex as the model developed by Coyle to help demonstrate some of the factors that influence endurance performance was, Saunders *et al.* (2004) proposed a significant number of factors that are likely to be influenced

by running economy (*see* Figure 1.5). They suggest that any training intervention that may aid in the reduction of oxygen cost for a range of running speeds and distances could, in turn, feasibly lead to improvements in running performance.

So, armed with some basic knowledge of the physiological factors that most impact on the ability to perform as a distance runner, and having an understanding that these components are part of a much bigger and far more complex jigsaw of a performance model, will give the athlete a clearer view of what training they need to improve performance.

# 2

# PRINCIPLES OF TRAINING

## So, you want to go faster?

Speaking to the BBC about British male distance runners in 2006, Dave Bedford stated:

> *Most of the youngsters on the men's side aren't doing nearly enough training or distance work . . . We used to train three times a day, 200 miles a week, and it's very clear that if you have that sort of commitment – and can stay clear of injury – then you will run very fast. But you have to be prepared to commit.*

Dave Bedford, Ron Hill and many others of their generation believed that the only way to get results as distance runners was to run as many miles as possible. While we can't argue with the results they achieved, we do disagree with Bedford's advice on training, especially in relation to club runners. Bedford's comment and Hill's commitment to training sum up the tradi-

tional attitude towards training which was a belief that only a high-volume regime would produce any significant results. And, for years, many club runners believed that if this approach worked for their heroes then it would work for them too. Go out and pile up the miles – and, if your results aren't what you expected, it must be because you are not training enough. So go out and do some more, even when you are ill or injured!

Of course, with advances in sports science we now know that such high-volume training will lead to improvement in those physically capable of enduring such training loads without over-training or ending up with over-use injuries. But, for ordinary club runners of lesser natural ability than elite athletes, it is often a recipe for disaster. For club athletes having to train after a hard day's work it is also folly to expect that they can expect to recover from each training session given that the elite athletes would have more time to rest after each day's training. While this may have been what Bedford endured, the value of rest and recovery is now much better understood.

The philosophy of this book is that more is not necessarily better – in fact, it is often worse. Bedford, Hill and others of their era were all incredible athletes, especially when you consider the sheer volume of racing and training they had to endure. However, injury and long periods of relative inactivity were also common. So, how much better would they have been had they had the benefit of modern training methods, recovery strategies and nutritional knowledge?

There's no point in a coach telling a runner to go out and run 120 miles a week if they are already exhausted trying to fit 80 miles of run training into a busy lifestyle, even if Bedford managed 200 miles. In this chapter we will outline the philosophy of our approach of tailored training to suit the needs of the individual. The old adage 'no pain, no gain' no longer applies. Yes, some of the training sessions we will suggest you do will be hard, and it will require focus and motivation to complete the schedule we will help you to construct, but we believe that the results will speak for themselves. The adage now is simply to 'train smart'.

## The building blocks of training

Before deciding on what training you need it is essential to first look at the demands of the

event you are facing. Every event is different, but there are some common elements to each. They are all endurance events requiring a large component of aerobic metabolism to underpin success. As an athlete or coach it is up to you to sit down and look at the event you have chosen to do, and consider the demands involved – for example, the impact of the hills in the Boston marathon, or the influence of the prevailing temperatures at the Comrades' Marathon, or the starting format of a national cross-country event. This is the start of the process of goal-setting.

The athlete should set her or himself short-, medium- and long-term goals. For an elite athlete, the long-term goal may be reaching the Olympic final in four years' time, with medium-term goals of national and world championships. For you, the long-term goal may be completing a marathon perhaps six or eight months away, or improving your 5 km performance in eight weeks' time. Medium-term goals may be other races prior to your main goal, used as training, as a way of assessing your progress, and perfecting pacing or nutritional strategy.

### Goal-setting

Many people find goal-setting difficult. It shouldn't be that way. Goals are best if they are clear and have measurable outcomes. These will not always be easy to achieve, but should be a stepping stone to the priority event, or long-term goals. Longer-terms goals may often be something like aiming to improve your performance time, your overall placing, or even just finishing a specific event. Medium-term goals may be trying to cover a certain distance in a training session, or achieving a certain amount of weight loss, while short-term goals will often focus on completing a certain amount of training within the next week, or even achieving heart rate targets for the training session that is just about to be undertaken.

Once you have set your long-term goal you can work backwards to decide how best to prepare to meet the challenge you have set yourself. Training has to be sport-specific – that is, you must prepare your body to cope with the demands made of it on race day. If your chosen event is a fast, flat 10 km there is great benefit in doing interval sessions at race pace or slightly faster – a concept alien to some improving runners, because these sessions 'hurt'. It may sound obvious, but it is a mistake many people make.

## Needs analysis

Take some time to think about the event you have entered. How far is it? How hilly will the event be? How steep will the climbs be? Also, what are the weather conditions likely to be? What about your nutritional requirements? Are you used to running in large groups of athletes? These are just a few of the factors that should be considered before preparing your training programme.

A needs analysis will help you answer all the above questions and put you on track for achieving your goals, whether these are to run for fun, health and fitness, or to compete on a regular basis at a high level.

The following areas will need to be addressed:

- Personal goals
- Training history
- Injury history
- Commitments (family, work, school, college, etc.)
- Time frame
- Equipment (running shoes, heart rate monitor, running gear, drinks bottle, night-time (reflective) running equipment, etc.)

These areas are quite simple to establish, will take a few minutes to address, and will outline a bit more clearly what kind of commitment you can give to your training and also what risk factors (e.g. injury history) you may have. Dealing with these issues ensures that you are prepared for the adventure and challenges ahead.

By completing a needs analysis form like the one shown in table 2.1, you can realistically calculate your weekly routine. It is also beneficial to discuss this with your family or partner first, so they know, for example, what you are doing in the evening three times a week, but also so they can become part of your support network. This is important in helping with adherence, especially when things get a bit more challenging, either though increased training load and frequency, or as the result of injury or when potential barriers arise (e.g. a new project at work that may demand more of your time and mean that your training gets put on hold). Having a support network is extremely beneficial during such times.

One of the key areas to address once you have established that you have the time, desire and support to run, is equipment. The most important bit of kit isn't the brand new running top that looks great, reflects in the dark and makes you feel like a pro – it is your running shoes! (This vital piece of equipment is discussed in Chapter 5.)

**Table 2.1 Example of a personal needs analysis**

| | |
|---|---|
| Name | John Smith |
| Date of needs analysis | 16 September 2009 |
| Personal goal/s | 1) Sub 3-hour marathon (pb by 7 minutes) at London, April 2010<br>2) 35-minute 10 km before New Year |
| Training history | Average of $4\frac{1}{2}$ hours per week, mostly steady/easy endurance since completing Ironman in July |
| Previous injuries | Tightness in ITB [iliotibial band]<br>Ankle surgery 18 months ago |
| Other commitments | Wife and two children . . . as well as work commitments – self-employed, so can have flexibility, but also can frequently be subject to last-minute change |
| What equipment do I need? | None additional at present, but current shoes at 270 miles of running |
| How often can I realistically train? | Probably 3 x a week with consistency, but need to make more of early-morning training |
| Other thoughts/points | Would like to try to maintain some cycling as enjoyment, if possible |

## The five key elements of training

An effective training programme has to have five different components, as discussed below.

### 1 Adequate volume

This is specific to the individual and dependent on how much time you can realistically devote to training. If you are a full-time professional, adequate volume may mean more than 20 hours per week. This is obviously a huge demand for a club runner with work and family commitments. That said, if you feel able to devote 10 hours per week to training it does not necessarily follow that this is the training volume you should aim for. If training for 10 hours per week leaves you over-trained and exhausted after a month then it serves no purpose to carry on with such a workload. There will, of course, be other athletes who only respond to higher volumes of training and are able to cope with this extra workload.

### 2 Appropriate duration

This means a training session duration appropriate to the intensity you are maintaining. For example, 'endurance zones' sessions should last around 60 to 90 minutes as this is the optimal duration for such a training intensity. Running at this intensity for longer won't produce greater physiological benefits – it's what many coaches refer to as the 'mile of diminishing returns'. There is a point in any training session where continuing won't bring any more significant gains, and will simply cause greater fatigue and delay the recovery process before your next training session.

### 3 Sufficient intensity

Everyone has been on a Sunday club run where the fast guys are cruising along at the front, happily chatting away to each other, while less talented runners are working hard, struggling for breath, just to desperately hold on to the back of the group. Training in groups like this is too easy for the elite or faster athletes, and far too hard for those looking to improve. Similarly, those 'steady runs' that turn into a race pace effort for the last three to four kilometres may not be what you need.

What is meant by sufficient intensity is that any training session has to be performed at a level appropriate to the duration and to the purpose of the session. There's little point doing a 20-minute run at a very low intensity unless it is specifically intended as a recovery session. Equally, going out on a club run and doing two hours at race pace with athletes far stronger than you is not the optimal way to improve fitness.

### 4 Sports specificity

Daft as it might sound, running is the best way to improve performance as a runner. There are many runners who will use other activities to stay in shape in the off-season, whether it's doing gym circuits or weight training. There may be some occasions where such work is necessary, particularly if an individual has a muscle imbalance or is recovering from injury. But the bulk of the training you do must be specific to the sport in which you wish to compete.

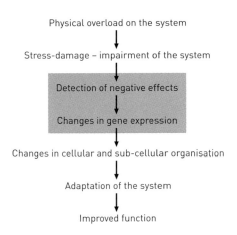

Physical overload on the system

↓

Stress-damage – impairment of the system

↓

Detection of negative effects

↓

Changes in gene expression

↓

Changes in cellular and sub-cellular organisation

↓

Adaptation of the system

↓

Improved function

**Figure 2.2 Model of training specificity**

Specificity is crucial when the factors in Figure 2.2 are considered. During exercise, a training stress, or stimulus, is placed on the body (physical overload) and the body becomes stressed, damaged or performance-impaired in some way. Although it is not possible to measure this (the area marked by the yellow box in Figure 2.2), as a result the body detects these negative effects, and in turn some changes in gene expression must happen. The resultant effect is that detectable changes in both cellular and sub-cellular organisation occur. These changes lead, in turn, to adaptation of the system, and ultimately improvement in performance. However, it must be remembered that the overload placed on the body will relate directly to the adaptation that occurs, so for specific adaptation to result, the overload needs to be specifically targeted.

## 5 Optimal recovery

Training promotes physiological changes to take place in the body, but it is during recovery that developments take place that make an individual better adapted to cope with the physical demands of racing. Without adequate recovery, these changes will not be completed before the next training session takes place. Lack of adequate recovery time will also lead to over-training and fatigue, which will prevent effective training development. Knowing when to rest, and for how long, is vital to developing an effective training programme.

## The overload principle

After a hard training session the body will be fatigued; it will have incurred some loss of carbohydrate energy stores and may even have suffered some minor muscle damage. If, for example, an average runner runs 16 km (10 miles) in 70 minutes and is fatigued afterwards, they may not be able to recover sufficiently to run the same route under the same conditions in the same time 24 hours later.

Consider Figure 2.3. Suppose an athlete starts a training session with 'fitness' at point A. Training suppresses the level of performance of which the body is capable. As the session progresses, fatigue results, and the 'fitness' or ability to perform is depressed to point B, where the training session ends. But give the body time to recover, and fitness will return to point C. Ultimately, given appropriate recovery and adequate nutrition, the body overcompensates by repairing muscle tissue and replacing carbohydrate stores to allow it to cope with this increased physical demand to point D. Should no further training take place, this increase in fitness will drop back to baseline (point E), or even below.

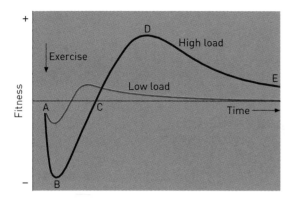

**Figure 2.3 The overload principle**

Over weeks and months, if this process is repeated and each session is started at the peak of recovery (point D), the body will show significant improvements in terms of the physical demand it is capable of coping with. This is how fitness improves through training. The key is to allow the body sufficient time to recover between training sessions so that the athlete avoids the damaging effects of over-training. If you continue to train before recovery is complete (somewhere between point B and C) you get a gradual decline in performance as opposed to a steady increase. This will soon lead to over-training.

## Basic periodisation

Most runners will be familiar with the idea of a training programme being described as a pyramid. Figure 2.4 shows how the base of the pyramid involves the lowest-intensity training and the highest volume. As you work your way

up the pyramid, the volume decreases as the intensity increases. We will employ a system of periodisation – that is to say, training will be split up into blocks building up to race day.

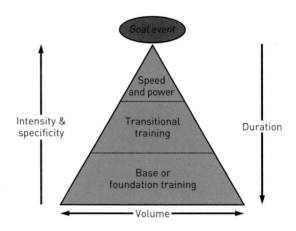

**Figure 2.4 Example of a training pyramid**

Before we start to determine how your training will be structured, you must first decide how much time you have available to train. There is little point in saying that you should do 12 hours of training a week if the demands of work and family life mean that you never have more than eight hours a week to train. Don't worry if you can manage to train for only four or five hours a week – you will be amazed at how much improvement can be made on such a programme.

Start by writing down your time commitments each week, including work, home life and leisure time (look back at table 2.1, if necessary, for an example of the sort of format to follow). Be honest with yourself and work out exactly how much time you have free to train each week. This is the starting point in building our schedule.

You also need to assess your own strengths and weaknesses. If you are a strong runner over a shorter distance but always struggle during the latter parts of a longer race this is an area you need to focus on. There may be other factors related to your performance – such as feeding strategies, pacing, hill-running technique or practising relaxed running – that will aid your performance. All such factors can affect your performance and need to be identified if they are weak areas. It's worth asking a coach or club mates to give you feedback on your own strengths and weaknesses, as they may spot things that you are not aware of.

From here we can begin to plan the training phases. Broadly speaking, the training programme will be structured as in the training pyramid diagram (Figure 2.4). It begins with a broad base of high-volume, low-intensity work, progressing to a transitional phase that intro-duces shorter, higher-intensity efforts. As race day approaches, volume decreases again while intensity is maintained. This is the broad picture, but within that we will have training cycles which involve weeks that build volume, followed by a week of recovery to allow the body to compensate for the effects of training and progress to a higher fitness level.

In the broad view illustrated by Figure 2.4, an endurance runner may focus as much as nine

months or as little as three months of work on improving their base fitness. The transitional training will then be a block of somewhere between six and twelve weeks (depending on the athlete's needs and ambitions) and will focus mostly on higher-intensity threshold work to develop race-pace ability. The final phase of speed and power is used for sharpening towards a key event. For the longer-distance endurance runner (marathon or ultra-marathon runner) this may be overlooked with little effect, but for the shorter-distance endurance athlete (5 km to 10 miles, or cross-country), this pace work will be a key facet of performance improvement. However, if your ambitions are to perform at your peak, and possibly also race, a block of two to six weeks can really give a jump in strength, and can be used effectively in tapering for a major event.

Some coaches advocate a stepped approach to progression of training load, as shown in Figure 2.5. Essentially, they suggest that, based on total training load (usually by looking at the product of training intensity with time), training will progress on a four-week cycle, the first and second weeks

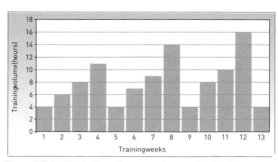

**Figure 2.5 An illustration of progressive overload and recovery used by some coaches**

being 'build' weeks, where the training is stepped up, and the third week being a training overload week; the fourth and final week of the phase is a recovery or regeneration week. The training cycle then repeats but with the volume of each week being slightly increased, so further progressive overload is applied.

In theory, this progressive overload will give perfect development, pushing the athlete forward, but also allowing for recovery. In practice, however, it takes all flexibility away from a training programme and can potentially lead to more problems than it solves. For example, what should an athlete do if at day 17 of the 21-day progression they become unwell; or how can the training programme be modified to compensate for severely inclement weather? For these reasons, we believe the best coaching strategy is to manage the athlete on a daily basis, to adjust training to the athlete's response, recovery, personal circumstances and the environmental conditions.

## Training with heart rate

Heart rate monitors have been around for years, yet there are still many runners who look at the numbers they show, but don't know how to use them properly. So why train using the heart rate as a guide at all? Elite athletes now use a combination of heart rate monitors and GPS systems to gauge their training intensity. GPSs are all the rage at the moment, but for the average runner a heart rate monitor is still the best training tool they can buy.

Heart rate gives a direct indication of the level of stress placed on the body at any given time. For around £40 you can get a monitor that is accurate enough to enable you to indicate changes in fitness, and even the onset of over-training or illness. But its most important function is its ability to determine training intensity. It will enable you to make the best use of the time you have available to train.

### Which heart rate monitor should I buy?

There are many heart rate monitors on the market, made by several reputable firms. Polar, being the originator of the commercially available heart rate monitor, is still considered to be the market leader, but there are many other manufacturers that make good-quality heart rate monitors. It is possible to pay more than £250 for a monitor that will allow you to download data, and will come with a highly technical software package that would be adequate for the use of an Olympic athlete and their coach or physiologist. However, for the average runner it may not be necessary to buy such an expensive monitor as you may never gain the full benefit of the functions it offers.

All you need is a good-quality monitor that is accurate and allows you to set upper and lower heart rate limits. Such a monitor will feature alarms that sound when your heart rate goes higher or lower than the limits you have set. This is important as you don't want to have to check your monitor display all the time. So a basic monitor will suffice, but if you are prepared to pay a little more, there are functions that are desirable but not essential.

Getting a heart rate monitor that allows data to be recorded at the end of a session means you can log your average heart rate and maybe the amount of calories burned during your training session. This data can be useful to assess how your fitness is improving and in helping you to lose weight.

### Determining maximum heart rate

Before any scientific training programme can begin, the physiologist or self-coached athlete must first determine their current state of fitness. Ideally, such an assessment would be carried out using a selection of physiological tests in a recognised sports laboratory. This is the type of testing used by Olympic-level athletes and elite runners to assess their current state of fitness, and a way of determining how their training should progress. Physiological testing in a sports science lab is desirable for an athlete wanting to make the most of their training time and to train scientifically, but not everyone reading this book will have the opportunity to undergo such a test. Therefore, we need to find another way of testing that, although not as accurate as a laboratory test, will provide data on which to base a scientific training programme.

At the very least we need to find out the athlete's maximum heart rate, through a physical test. Many books recommend theoretical formulas for calculating maximum heart rate based on the athlete's age, but these can be wildly inaccurate. So we will ask you to carry out your own test, which we can then use to determine training zones. Whether done in a sports science lab or by self-testing, determining maximum heart rate is hard work for the athlete – it involves an all-out effort, so there are a few things to consider before proceeding.

## Risks of exercising

While the risks of undertaking a fitness test may be no greater than participating in a race, our professional responsibility means that we encourage everyone who undertakes an exercise test or begins a training programme, even if self-led, to complete a physical activity readiness questionnaire (PAR-Q).

The original PAR-Q was developed by the British Columbia Ministry of Health. It has been revised by an Expert Advisory Committee of the Canadian Society for Exercise Physiology chaired by Dr N. Gledhill (2002). It is an excellent tool, which is recognised worldwide as an effective screen for individuals aged between 15 and 69 years of age, prior to them starting an exercise programme. A copy of the PAR-Q can be found at www.csep.ca/communities/c574/files/hidden/pdfs/par-q.pdf.

If you answer 'Yes' to one or more questions, then you should see your doctor prior to starting your exercise programme. The form is valid for up to a year, as long as your situation doesn't change. If any of your answers change from 'No' to 'Yes', you should seek medical advice before continuing with your conditioning programme.

However, for a healthy, injury-free individual, the maximum heart rate test is perfectly safe to undertake. If you have health problems (that you may be aware of or that have been highlighted by the PAR-Q) or are returning to exercise after a long period of inactivity, you may wish to check with your GP before proceeding. In particular, if you or members of your family have a history of heart problems, you may also wish to seek medical advice first. If you are fit and healthy and are a regular runner the test will be no more demanding than a hard training session or short-distance race. Due to motivational factors associated with competing against other athletes, some individuals will find they may achieve maximum heart rates higher during a competitive event than they do in a structured test.

Having dealt with the health advice before taking the test we must now take into account some other considerations to make sure we get the most accurate result possible. Before taking the maximum heart rate test the athlete must:

- be in a rested condition, ideally in the same rested condition as they would be prior to a big race; testing should, ideally, take place at least 48 hours after the last bout of heavy training;
- be fully hydrated and have a good level of carbohydrate stores;
- have performed a warm-up;
- use their usual training or competition equipment.

## Self-administered treadmill test

While running outside, the effects of the wind will help with cooling and so dissipate heat. When you are running on a treadmill, however, this mechanism of cooling is greatly reduced, and heat builds up, causing excessive sweating. This causes the heart to beat faster and can affect the result of the maximum heart rate test, so get a fan to keep you cool.

You will also need to be wearing your heart monitor and to check that it is picking up your heartbeat before starting. Ideally, your monitor will have a record function that will allow you to view data from the test when it is over. Remember, you need to find your maximum heart rate, so make sure your heart rate monitor records this data. If it doesn't have a record function, you will need to remember to check your heart rate immediately at the end of the test to see the highest figure achieved. Additionally, it may be worth asking a friend to keep an eye on it while you concentrate on running (if you use this approach, your friend should stand holding the heart rate monitor just behind your back).

Make sure you have performed a satisfactory warm-up and completed your usual pre-training routine. Although this test may be short, it can get very intense. Give yourself at least 10 minutes of gentle running at a speed considerably easier than your usual running pace. Depending on your ability, this could be as low as 6 km/h or as high at 14 km/h (target marathon pace less 2 km/h is a good starting point to try from). We would also recommend that, where possible, the treadmill gradient is set to 1 per cent as this better reflects running on the road. Make sure you are running in as relaxed a way as possible, and in your normal stride pattern. Follow this with a few minutes' break and a light stretch if you are used to pre-exercise stretching.

Start the test running at this same pace for a further minute. To save you looking at a stop-watch and having to control the treadmill by yourself, it may be worth getting a friend to help. At the end of this minute, increase the treadmill speed by 0.5 km/h. As each 30 seconds passes, you have to increase the speed by 0.5 km/h until you are no longer able to maintain the pace. At this point dismount safely by either using the stop button or holding on to the handrails and stepping off the treadmill belt.

Your heart should now be working at its maximum and the test is complete. After a few minutes' rest, you can warm down by gently jogging for a further 5–10 minutes. While the main objective of this test is to determine maximum heart rate, you can also record the maximum speed achieved during the test. If in future months you perform the same test, you can use the results to identify improvements in fitness.

If you are not used to running on a treadmill, or are not confident about running at speed on the treadmill, a form of field-based testing may be more advisable.

## Field testing

Field testing is the generic term used to describe any non-laboratory-based fitness test. Many of these testing methods can be self-administered, and therefore can potentially benefit a runner in tracking changes in their fitness levels. Many of them can be undertaken with groups, so they are sometimes used by running club coaches on a seasonal basis to monitor the progression of a training group or athlete within that group.

It is important when completing any type of fitness testing that certain guidelines are adhered to in order for the assessments to be accurate. Specificity of training comes in to play with testing. A specific test will replicate the physiological requirements of a particular sport or activity. There is no point performing a medicine ball throw to analyse power output if you are a 1500 m runner!

In addition to being specific, to ensure that a test is providing accurate information on which you can depend, each test must be valid, reliable and objective. This applies whether you are performing your test under laboratory conditions or in the field.

### Validity of testing

A good test must be valid. This means that it will provide useful and meaningful results, and that it measures what it claims to measure! Often you may choose a battery of tests for team sports as there may be a number of components of fitness that lead to success in that particular sport. For example, as a runner, you may choose an endurance test in addition to a test for strength and power (for the sprint at the end). Each sport and discipline will have slightly different specifics, which will mean that the validity will need to be considered.

## Reliability

This relates to the consistency of the results over repeated testing. For example, if you were to conduct a speed test over 30 m with a stopwatch compared to timing gates, then the timing gates would lead to the test being much more reliable than the measure with the stopwatch. This reliability is compromised even more if a different person timed you during each testing phase: human error is a big factor in reliability. We now have the technology to measure much more accurately, thereby increasing the reliability of the test results.

The following can all affect the reliability of a test:

- Standardised warm-up
- Number of trials
- Rest between trials
- Personnel recording the test
- Instrumentation used
- Test familiarity
- Individual motivation

- Protocol selection (was it the same protocol the last time you were tested?)

The above all need to be considered and outlined before completing a field test. There should be documented, standardised procedures in order to increase the reliability of the test for future testing and accurate comparison.

Such things as testing surface, time of day of the test, participant fatigue, nutrition and hydration are all variables that can be controlled. There will be uncontrollable factors during field testing – for example, the weather – that may affect the results, and this has to be considered and noted during the test so that subsequent assessments can be compared as thoroughly and as accurately as possible.

## Objectivity

This is the measure of degree of agreement between two or more different testers on a particular test. For example, if two different people administered the same test at different times, they should produce similar or, preferably, identical results with the same person being tested (based on the individual being fully recovered and not experiencing any further training effect).

A good example of this within field testing is the multi-stage fitness test. The test criteria state that an individual should be stopped if they miss the bleep on more than two consecutive turns. If one administrator adhered to these criteria but another allowed the individual to continue, then it would affect the objectivity of the test and subsequently become an invalid result.

This is frustrating for the individual being tested as the whole point of fitness testing is to gain an objective measure of the particular effectiveness of training during a particular phase, and to set realistic goals. This will all be invalid if the test is not performed to the appropriate criteria or protocol and subsequent objectivity.

As you can see from all the tests listed in table 2.2, one of the main limitations is participant motivation and effort. If the participant fails to complete the test to the best of their ability, or maximally, then this will affect the results. You cannot hide on the treadmill or in laboratory-based tests, as accurate physiological measurements will be assessed throughout the process. One of the limiting factors with field-based testing is the effort and motivation of the participants.

**Table 2.2 Examples of valid, reliable and objective field tests specific to runners**

| Test | Physiological component tested | Main limitations | Main strengths |
|---|---|---|---|
| Multi-stage fitness test (bleep test) | Aerobic endurance | Requires maximum effort | Reliable test Provides prediction of an individual's $VO_2max$ |
| Half-mile run | | Requires maximum effort, also requires effective pacing and can be affected by the weather | Reliable test Provides prediction of an individual's $VO_2max$ |
| 12-minute run | | Requires maximum effort, also requires effective pacing and can be affected by the weather | Reliable test Provides prediction of an individual's $VO_2max$ |

**Table 2.2 Examples of valid, reliable and objective field tests specific to runners (cont.)**

| Test | Physiological component tested | Main limitations | Main strengths |
|---|---|---|---|
| Kosmin test | Aerobic endurance | Requires maximum effort and high motivation, as well as accurate measurement by the test administrator | Predicts the runner's 800 m and 1500 m times High correlation to competition performance |
| Selection of 10 m, 30 m, 40 m acceleration tests | Speed and acceleration | Requires maximum effort and high motivation | Can have a high correlation with potential performance in competition with experienced athletes |
| Vertical jump test | Power | Requires maximum effort and high motivation | A good indicator of explosive power, which correlates highly with the development of speed and acceleration |

The athlete has to have a level of preparedness in order for the test to reflect their current level of fitness and conditioning, especially when re-testing occurs to ensure an accurate comparison, with all things taken into consideration. Ideally, the athlete must be responsible for the following:

- Level of motivation (maximal effort)
- Nutrition
- Hydration
- Level of fatigue (sleep, rest and recovery, and any physical activity completed the day before the test, will affect this component)

## The benefits of physiological testing

The effects of many of the issues listed above should be reduced in laboratory tests, and athletes keen to get a full understanding of their physiology will choose this route of assessment. The treadmill test or field tests outlined above to determine your maxlmum heart rate will give you the ability to target your training, and offer a way of measuring the intensity of your sessions when you run. It is a scientific approach that will bring benefits and help you make the most of the time you have available to train. But there are things that these tests will not do. While the method we have outlined is a good place to start, there are advantages to be had from undergoing a full physiological assessment at a reputable sports science laboratory.

**Figure 2.6 Physiological testing in progress**

Ideally, fitness testing sessions should include an assessment of body fat – to give body fat percentage and help set nutritional targets (including target carbohydrate, protein and fat intakes), to aid weight loss (where required) or enhance recovery from training. Running-specific test protocols then enable assessment of fitness by determination (through measurement rather than prediction) of maximal oxygen uptake ($VO_2$max), maximum heart rate, heart rate training zones, peak running speed, anaerobic threshold and sub-maximal $VO_2$ to determine running economy.

These are all factors that affect your performance. The results of the fitness tests and nutrition assessment can then be used to determine your strengths and weaknesses during running. This information can be used to provide specific training advice, allowing you to train smarter, and ultimately to improve your training and racing performance. Testing gives you an indication of your current physiological status, outlining your strengths and weaknesses. Repeat testing allows you to monitor your progress. Performance in training and competition can indicate how well an athlete performs, but not the reasons why. To get the most from the tests, it is important to use medically accurate apparatus and sport-specific scientific methods to assess why you are performing as you are, allowing you and/or your coach to adjust your training programmes accordingly. In addition to standard testing services, biomechanical and psychological support and intervention can also be considered if this is a key weakness in your performance.

Up until a few years ago, all this was available only to an elite few on Olympic programmes or in professional teams. You can still make significant performance gains without physiological testing if you follow the guidelines in this book, but if you want to achieve the best possible performance then a full physiological assessment would be a good place to start.

## BENEFITS OF FITNESS TESTING

In addition to providing values for undertaking training, fitness testing will help you:

- to highlight possible strengths and weaknesses within your individual fitness profile;
- as a baseline from which to monitor your return to fitness after an injury, illness or time off;
- make an objective evaluation of the effectiveness of a particular training programme or phase of training;
- to set appropriate training goals for fitness development;
- by encouraging adherence and motivation towards your training programme;
- provide individual feedback regarding your progress towards your fitness goals;
- increase motivation via goal-setting.

## What the numbers mean

Figure 2.7 shows the results of a physiological assessment. The first 15-minute period of the test is a sub-maximal test. Following a light warm-up and stretch, the athlete undertakes three five-minute periods of increasing intensity, with the workloads selected to reflect the runner's fitness and ability. It would be expected that the final workload in the sub-maximal protocol would elicit a response very close to threshold.

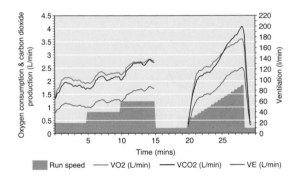

**Figure 2.7 Physiological test results**

Oxygen uptake (the blue line) is measured continuously throughout the sub-maximal test. The primary value of these measures is to monitor changes with training; however, they are also used to determine running economy and fuel utilisation rate. Economy, as we learned earlier, is determined by the amount of oxygen needed to run at a given speed, and will be impacted by poor metabolic processes or inefficient biomechanics.

After a further five-minute rest period, a progressive maximal test is undertaken.

Workloads are designed to gradually increase at a rate suitable for the individual's ability. Again, breathing is monitored throughout, and the graph shows the linear increase in oxygen uptake ($VO_2$) as a blue line, as the workload is increased over time. The waste gas carbon dioxide ($VCO_2$) is also monitored and its production is illustrated as a red line.

Significantly, where the athlete is working aerobically, and able to use both fat and carbohydrate as a fuel, the blue line ($VO_2$) will be above the red line ($VCO_2$). The point of threshold occurs when the two lines come together; this also represents the use of 100 per cent carbohydrate as a fuel. Where the red line ($VCO_2$) is above the blue ($VO_2$), this demonstrates that the athlete is working anaerobically to maintain the load. In some cases it can take several minutes to reach equilibrium, hence the values at the end of each steady period are observed in the sub-maximal test.

The results of these and similar tests can then be used to determine training zones that are far more specific to your current fitness and individual heart rate responses.

## The training zones

So, we now have data on the athlete's maximum heart rate and speed at $VO_2$max. Using this figure, we can now determine heart rate training zones to develop different areas of fitness. We will be working with five training zones, based on principles established by Peter Keen, the former performance director at British

Cycling, to explain the physiological approach to our training programme. Some coaches and physiologists use six or seven zones, but the principles of training specific muscle groups for a specific purpose remain the same.

Please note that, although we have applied estimated heart rates, these are not wholly accurate as changes in running economy may occur with changes in running speed, the surface on which the athlete is running, and also changes in running style.

### Recovery/base (R&B) training

Steady-state long-distance running is undertaken at a very low intensity. Sessions at this intensity could be maintained for three hours or more. The limiting factors are adequate supplies of fluid, and energy from carbohydrate.

In training for longer-distance endurance races, sessions at this low intensity are only of real use in getting the body used to exercising for long periods. Such low-intensity running is the type many runners have used for years, believing that 'getting the miles in' was the only way to achieve optimum fitness. Such a traditional, non-scientific approach was based on the belief that more was better: if 200 kilometres (125 miles) a week was followed by a race win, then 320 kilometres (200 miles) a week would produce even better results!

Of course, we now know that such a system may allow some runners to perform well, but most will end up over-trained and fatigued.

Running at this intensity will be used in our training programme to allow athletes to adapt to long hours on their feet and, in much shorter sessions, to allow for recovery from a heavy training session. As a guide, sessions at this level should be performed at heart rates of at least 45 beats per minute (bpm) below your maximum, so if your maximum is 190 you should not exceed 145 bpm at this level.

## Endurance (END) training

As a distance runner, this is the key session in your programme. You will do more endurance work than anything else, in order to optimise your performance. Endurance training sessions are significantly more intense than the recovery/base training level, but are not 'flat out' efforts. The feeling should be the same as that you would experience during a steady run, certainly much easier than you would feel during a longer race. Ideally, if you were running with a small group, you would need to concentrate on your pace, and would be able to have a conversation with another athlete, but would need to take a deep and full breath, probably between each sentence. If the conversation becomes free-flowing, you are running too easily. If the pace increases so that you can no longer maintain the conversation, you are probably running a little too fast. Sessions at this intensity need only last for approximately 40 minutes, although ideally they will be between 60 and 90 minutes, but could, infrequently, be extended to two hours or slightly longer.

It is possible to train at this intensity for longer, but the potential muscle damage caused by doing so outweighs any extra benefits gained. The idea is to be able to stress the body enough to prompt a training response without causing so much fatigue that it takes two or three days to recovery sufficiently to be able to resume training at the same intensity.

This level of training is important because it promotes significant improvements in both cardiovascular and energy efficiency. These sessions require significant amounts of carbohydrate, so carbohydrate drinks or gels must be used if the sessions are to be completed successfully. This level of training uses the slow-twitch (type 1) aerobic muscle fibre, which is essential to train for improved endurance. Essentially it is a fat-burning fibre, although in endurance training sessions you will be using a significant amount of carbohydrate too. If you are predicting your training zones from your maximum heart rate, training at this level should be done at between 35 and 45 bpm below your maximum. So, if your maximum heart rate is 190 bpm, you should run at between 145 and 155 bpm.

## Mixed muscle zone (MMZ)

This is a zone in between the endurance zone and threshold zone. Research undertaken by one of the authors (Dr Palmer) suggests that the MMZ uses a mix of both the slow- (type 1) and fast-twitch aerobic (type 2a) muscle fibres used in the endurance and threshold zones. Our training programme will not target training in this zone as it is not going to produce the specific benefits needed to improve your performance for endurance running, especially when you have limited training time available to you. We mention this zone, however, as it is commonly the zone in which many athletes end up training.

Training in this zone will bring some fitness benefits, but they will not be as rapid as the benefits of targeted training in the endurance and threshold zones. This mixed muscle zone will fatigue both endurance type 1 muscle fibres and threshold type 2a muscle fibres. One of the benefits of targeting endurance and threshold fibres on separate days is that it allows the muscle fibres more opportunity to recover between training sessions, and this is lost by training in this zone. When training in the endurance zone the muscle fibres used for threshold training are getting a chance to recover, and vice versa. This is especially important if you reconsider Figure 2.3, showing the impact of training overload and recovery.

## Threshold training (ThT)

Sessions at this intensity are important for the distance runner as they will improve race-pace work. Threshold sessions are at an intensity that is on a par with a 10 km to 16 km (6- to 10-mile) race effort. They can be performed on a track or a flat section of road, but equally can also be undertaken on a gradual climb or even on a treadmill. These sessions will be continuous efforts of between 20 and 30 minutes, or extended interval repetitions of between 3 and

12 minutes. They will improve your lactic acid tolerance and enable you to sustain greater race-pace for shorter-distance events, or give greater strength on gradual climbs.

This level of effort involves the fast-twitch oxidative (type 2a) muscle fibres, which require large amounts of oxygen to function properly. The feeling a runner should have at this intensity is of a hard, but not flat-out, effort. Breathing should be rhythmic and deep, and the athlete would not be able to hold a conversation during this level of effort. You should be able to respond to a question with a one- or two-word answer, but that's about all. Sessions at this level should be done at a rate of between an estimated 15 and 25 bpm below your maximum. So, if your maximum heart rate is 190 bpm, you should run at between 165 and 175 bpm.

## Speed and power (S&P) training

This is the icing on the cake: short, high-intensity interval training designed to provide the finishing touches in the final weeks before a big event. Such sessions involve maximum effort with relatively long recovery periods. Athletes completing longer-distance events, such as a marathon, may not need this sort of training, but it may still have benefits. For those athletes looking to race over the shorter-distance endurance events (5 km and 10 km) and cross-country races, this element of training will be vital in giving additional strength, and a burst of speed and power when needed.

This type of effort involves the use of the fast-twitch, glycolytic (type 2b) muscle fibres, which do not require the use of oxygen to function. They come into play in a sprint, or when the athlete is fatigued and simply cannot take in oxygen quickly enough to supply the anaerobic muscle fibres. Type 2b fibres cause a large increase in lactic acid production, leading to rapid onset of fatigue. Sessions at this level should be done at a heart rate within 15 bpm below your maximum, so if your maximum heart rate is 190 bpm, you should train above 175 bpm – although when doing these sessions, if you look to apply maximum effort, heart rate will not be a factor.

## Training effectively

It is vitally important that, in each session, you try to maintain your heart rate within the specified training zones. If your endurance zone heart rate is 145–155 bpm, then you must set the limits on your heart monitor to alert you as to when you are moving in and out of this zone.

Some heart rate monitors will tell you what your average heart rate was at the end of a training session. This can be misleading. For example, say you had an average heart rate reading of 150 bpm after an hour-long training run. This would seem fine if you were the athlete with a heart rate range of 145–155 bpm for an endurance session. But if that athlete spent the first 30 minutes exercising at 130 bpm and the last 30 minutes at 170 bpm, then they would have spent virtually no time at all in the specified zone. Your aim should be to spend as much of your training

session as possible within your recommended zone.

Out on the road, your heart rate may vary due to terrain or having to stop at road junctions, etc. As the terrain changes, you should try to adjust your running speed and stride length to keep your heart rate at the right level. During an endurance run that means slowing down when you get to a steep hill, and trying to increase stride length and run faster on a descent. If you have to stop at a road junction or crossing, you should aim initially to keep jogging on the spot to maintain your heart rate a little, and then to accelerate gradually until your heart rate increases and gets back within the target zone. Remember, the key to this training programme is that it targets specific muscle groups to gain specific physiological benefits.

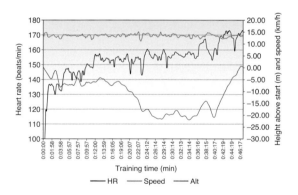

**Figure 2.8 An example of a heart rate trace observed when a runner is undertaking a non-structured training session**

If you are on an endurance run and your heart rate drops too low there is no point in sprinting away to get your heart rate back up into the target zone. Doing that will involve using the type 2b fast-twitch sprint fibres. This interrupts the stress being placed on the endurance fibres and it may take the body 15 to 20 minutes to clear the anaerobic backlog and fully bring the endurance fibres back into most effective use. If you constantly switch between using different types of muscle fibre you will not initiate the physiological changes we want to promote for improved fitness.

Figure 2.8 shows a classic example of a runner training with a focus on pace. As can clearly be seen there are massive fluctuations in their heart rate response. While this athlete main-tains their objective of averaging between 150 and 160 bpm for the duration of the 45-minute run, only 40 per cent was spent in the correct training zone. That's 60 per cent of the session wasted, or where the athlete could have been working more effectively or doing other things.

Figure 2.9 shows the training approach we are advocating. It is not easy to achieve, but in this case the athlete spends over 90 per cent of

their time in the correct training zone. This is achieved by them decreasing pace on climbs and working harder on descents. This makes the session far more effective. It also means that if we again consider the principle of training overload (Figure 2.3), the athlete can work in a different intensity zone on the next training session, thereby maximising the recovery time of that particular group of muscle fibres recruited in the training.

In addition to the steady-state training methods that we prescribe, some runners may add func-tional fitness sessions to develop abilities such as hill running, or to aid the development of running form and strength endurance. These will be discussed in subsequent chapters.

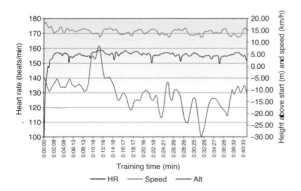

Figure 2.9 An example of how the work profile should be when an athlete is focusing on training intensity using heart rate

# 2

# INJURY PREVENTION

# 3

# FLEXIBILITY AND STRETCHING: CONCEPTS AND RATIONALE

Many runners underestimate the benefits of stretching, or are unsure about which stretches they should be doing, when they should do them and for how long they should stretch. The rationale and research behind each stretching technique will be discussed here to provide practical guidelines that you can apply to your daily training routine.

## The benefits of stretching

Regular stretching is a powerful part of any exercise programme, with the following benefits:

- Increased flexibility: flexible muscles can improve your daily performance in every day tasks as well as in your running programme.
- Improved range of motion for your joints: a good range of motion keeps you in

better balance, which will help keep you mobile and less prone to injury as your limbs pass through an increased range of movement, as they do during exercise.
- Improved circulation: stretching increases blood flow to your muscles; improved circulation can speed recovery after muscle injury and exercise.
- Promotes better posture: frequent stretching keeps your muscles from getting tight, allowing you to maintain proper posture, and minimising aches and pains.
- Stress relief: stretching relaxes the tense muscles that often accompany stress.
- May help prevent injury: preparing your muscles and joints for activity can protect you from injury, especially if your muscles or joints are tight.

There are a number of different types of stretches; all have a specific purpose in relation to your exercise programme. Choosing to perform each type at the appropriate time will help reduce injury potential and enhance performance. In the following sections we discuss the main types of stretching and the rationale for when they should be implemented.

## Static stretching

Static stretching (*see* Figure 3.1) involves gradually easing in to the stretch position and holding the position.

The amount of time for which a static stretch is held depends on your objectives. If it is part of your cool-down then stretches should be held for no longer than 10 seconds because of the micro-tears in the muscles, with the goal being to realign the muscle fibres and help pump out any waste products resulting from the exercise session.

Often in static stretching you are advised to move further into the stretch position as the stretch sensation subsides, to increase your range of movement (ROM). This would be advisable for 'developmental flexibility', which is when you want to improve muscle length, but not for the cool-down.

If your goal is, however, to improve your range of motion and muscle length, then hold the stretch for up to 30 seconds (developmental flexibility) and perform this on a separate

occasion (not after intense training), with the specific aim of increasing muscular range of motion.

You should be warm when you do this type of stretching as this will decrease the viscosity of the joints and increase circulation, which is a more productive environment for improving your joints' range of movement. You can complete static stretching for developmental flexibility after a lighter session, when muscle soreness is not a consideration.

**Figure 3.1 Static stretches: hamstrings, quads, glutes**

Research by Yamaguchi *et al.* (2006) has demonstrated that there is a loss in power output from the muscle if a stretch is held for too long prior to exercise, as in static stretching. His research used a protocol of 4 x 30-second holds with six types of static stretches. With sport, and running in particular, being a dynamic, powerful event, then a loss in power output is not desirable; for this reason, athletes should not perform static stretches with holds up to 30 seconds, prior to exercise.

**Figure 3.1 (cont.) Static stretches: calves, hip flexors, groins**

## Dynamic flexibility

Dynamic flexibility consists of controlled leg and arm swings, and movement patterns that take you gently to the limits of your range of motion. You should complete dynamic flexibility movements before any type of exercise.

Dynamic flexibility, in addition to working up to the muscle's functional ROM, has the added benefit of increasing body temperature, and increasing heart rate and breathing rate in order to prepare the body for exercise. The stretches should be held for no longer than three or four seconds, to ensure that the movement remains 'dynamic'.

**Figure 3.2  Dynamic flexibility: hamstring flicks, groins (internal and external)**

Figure 3.2 (cont.) Dynamic flexibility: groins (sideways), hip flexors, quads, high knees

Functional movement patterns (*see* Figure 3.2) that mimic the movements of the sport can be done within the warm-up and as part of dynamic flexibility – for example, hamstring flicks in order to warm up the hamstrings, which will also dynamically stretch the quadriceps muscles.

## PNF technique

Proprioceptive neuromuscular facilitation (PNF) involves the use of a muscle contraction before the stretch in an attempt to achieve maximum muscle relaxation and an increased stretch response. It is a partner-assisted exercise and can be used to increase the ROM of the muscle (*see* the example in Figure 3.3).

You complete PNF stretching as follows:

1. Move into the stretch position so that you feel the stretch sensation.
2. Your partner holds the limb in this stretched position.
3. You then push against your partner by contracting the antagonistic muscles for 6–10 seconds, and then relax. During the contraction, your partner aims to resist any movement of the limb.
4. Your partner then moves the limb further into the stretch until you feel the stretch sensation.
5. Go back to step 2. (Repeat this procedure three or four times before the stretch is released.)

**Figure 3.3 PNF hamstring stretch**

# Myofascial release

Myofascial release is a very effective hands-on technique that provides sustained pressure into myofascial restrictions to eliminate pain and restore movement. Fascia (*see* Figure 3.4) is strong connective tissue that performs a number of functions, including enveloping and isolating the muscles of the body, and providing structural support and protection. Underneath the superficial fascia lies deep fascia, in a much more

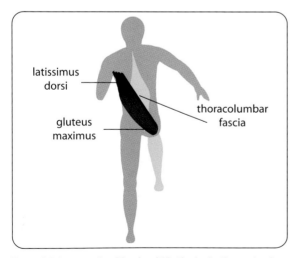

**Figure 3.4 An example of fascia within the body: thoracolumbar fascia of the back.**

densely packed and strong layer. Deep fascia covers the muscles in connective tissue, which help to keep them divided and protected. On occasion, this fascia can create tight knots or connective adhesions, which act as trigger points that can cause pain.

Myofascial release is a type of soft tissue massage that incorporates stretching and massage of the connective tissues or fascia. According to practitioners of myofascial release, poor posture, injury, illness and stress can negatively affect body alignment and cause fascia to become restricted. They believe that this can cause pain and impair movement. A gentle form of stretching and manual compression is said to restore flexibility to this connective tissue, and provide relief from fascial restrictions and pain. Myofascial release aims to access these trigger points, thereby freeing up the muscle and allowing it to move more easily and effectively. Trigger points have been defined as areas of muscle that are painful to palpation and are characterised by the presence of what seem like knots within the muscle.

It is possible to effectively perform myofascial release self-massage or stretch with the use of a tennis ball or foam roller (*see* Figure 3.5). You should move the foam roller or tennis ball around the particular body part until you feel some discomfort – this is the trigger point. You should hold the roller or ball there until the muscle relaxes; this may take up to 30–45 seconds, or until the pain has gone. Resume rolling until you find another trigger point. Stop

## MYOFASCIAL RELEASE: THE SCIENCE

A simple review of neuromuscular anatomy is required to apply the neurophysiological concepts of myofascial release.

Two basic neural receptors are located in skeletal muscle tissue. These receptors are the muscle spindle and the golgi tendon organ (GTO). *Muscle spindles* are located parallel to the muscle fibres. They record changes in fibre length, and rate of change to the central nervous system (CNS). This triggers the myotatic stretch reflex, which reflexively shortens muscle tissue, alters the normal length/tension relationship and often induces pain. GTOs are located at the musculotendinous junction within a muscle. They are sensitive to change in tension and rate of tension change. Stimulation of the GTOs past a certain threshold inhibits the muscle spindle activity and decreases muscular tension. This phenomenon is referred to as *autogenic inhibition*. It is said to be 'autogenic' because the contracting agonist is inhibited by its own receptors. Reduction in soft-tissue tension decreases pain, restores normal muscle length/tension relationships and improves function.

and hold again until the pain goes. A treatment can take as long as you want – usually, between five and ten minutes is sufficient. It is an ongoing method, though, so persevere!

Self-myofascial release is excellent before training as it relaxes the muscles and helps reduce trigger points, which will allow the muscle to move more freely.

## Factors limiting flexibility

There are a number of factors that can limit flexibility and the range of movement of a joint.

**Figure 3.5 Myofascial release: ITB, Calf**

**Figure 3.5 (cont.) Myofascial release: hamstring, quads, glutes (piriformis)**

## Internal influences

- Type of joint
- Internal resistance within a joint
- Bony structures that limit movement
- Temperature of the joint and associated tissues
- Elasticity of muscle tissue, tendons, ligaments and skin
- Ability of a muscle to relax and contract to achieve the greatest ROM

## External influences

- Temperature of the place where one is training (a warmer temperature is more conducive to increased flexibility)
- Time of day (most people are more flexible in the afternoon than in the morning)
- Stage in the recovery process of a joint (or muscle)
- Age (pre-adolescents are generally more flexible than adults)
- Gender (females are generally more flexible than males)
- Restrictions of any clothing or equipment
- One's ability to perform a particular exercise
- One's commitment to achieving flexibility

## Stretching plan: practical application

An example of a stretching plan is shown in table 3.1.

It is important to consider a balance in one's flexibility: you need both strength and flexibility. Strengthening (concentric) will shorten a muscle – for example, you can tell when someone just 'pumps out' on the bench press because they have rounded shoulders as their pectorals have shortened because of the movement pattern of the bench press. If the athlete stretches their pectorals after performing the bench press then muscle length will be regained. Also, if a joint is hyper-mobile then it may be sensible to strengthen the muscles around the joints to reduce this hyper-mobility.

**Table 3.1 Example of a stretching plan**

| Stretching modality | When? | Duration of holds | Purpose |
|---|---|---|---|
| **Dynamic flexibility** | Warm-up | 3–5 seconds | Prepare the muscles for training, working through a functional ROM |
| **Static** | Cool-down | 5–10 seconds | Muscle fibre realignment and aid in the dissipation of waste products after the exercise session |
| **Developmental flexibility (static)** | After a light training session or when warm | 2–3 x 30 seconds per exercise | To increase muscle length |
| **PNF** | After a light training session or when warm | 3–4 x 6–10 seconds per exercise | To increase muscle length and maximum muscular relaxation |
| **Myofascial release** | Pre- or post-training | 30–45 seconds, or until the pain has gone (once the trigger point has been found) | Muscle relaxation and reduction in trigger points and fascial restrictions |

# 4

# OVER-TRAINING, INJURY PREVENTION AND PERFORMANCE

One major issue that often besets athletes of all abilities is that they are goal driven. They have a set target, and they will do everything to achieve it. Some blindly follow training regimens from their favourite running magazine, or recommended on the internet, while others just have to get that extra mile in to ensure they are ready on race day. Sport can be all-consuming, and sometimes knowing when to stop is as important as knowing when to push. This is often when illness or injury strikes, so just what could and should be done about it?

## Evaluation of progress

By giving yourself baseline measures, any specific weaknesses that may lead to injury will be highlighted. An awareness of training history,

goals, injury history, correct equipment, running surface and how your body functions all add up to a successful, injury-free training and conditioning phase.

However, once you begin your training and conditioning, with the increased load and perhaps unaccustomed to exercise, you may well be more susceptible to injury and illness. The most important thing to do when you begin your training is to listen to your body: it will tell you when it feels good and also when it feels like a rest! Don't feel guilty if you don't feel on top of the world one day and miss a run; it is most probably your body telling you, physically, that it needs a rest, rather than anything to do with your lack of adherence or motivation.

Having an awareness of training load (the frequency, intensity and also the duration of your session) is important in establishing an effective and safe training regime. By completing a training log, you will be able to track these parameters – frequency, intensity and time – to provide you with what is known as the FIT principle. This is the foundation of an effective and measured training programme. It allows the individual to monitor and record their training load week by week, and track any changes by virtue of the fact that what they are doing is documented. Along with daily resting heart rate data, it can be a valuable tool.

With the FIT principle, frequency is the number of sessions each week, time is purely the duration of the activity, and intensity is how hard you are working during the sessions. Intensity can be subjectively measured via the 'rating of perceived exertion' (RPE) scale. In addition to high-tech devices like GPS and heart rate monitoring, it can help to use the RPE scale as it is an effective tool, which allows the athlete, as well as coaches, strength and conditioning instructors, physiotherapists and other exercise professionals, to monitor the subjective intensity of a particular session or training day. While measures like heart rate and GPS will provide objective measures for the athlete and coaches, the RPE scale will provide a subjective measure that is useful in helping to piece together training load and intensity.

The RPE scale is found in two forms. The original 0–20 rating scale (Nobel et al., 1983), has been adapted and revised to the Borg Category Ratio (CR10) scale, described below (Borg, 1998). Either scale is appropriate as a subjective tool for exercisers. Both scales were developed to allow the exerciser to subjectively rate his or her feelings during exercise, taking into account personal fitness level, environmental conditions and general fatigue levels (Nobel et al., 1983).

The CR10 scale is a means to produce estimates of exertion that would be comparable across people and across tasks. These scales are now commonly used in exercise testing, training and rehabilitation settings. It is important to use standardised instructions in order to reduce misinterpretation of the RPE scale. The following instructions are recommended for using the RPE during exercise testing:

*During the exercise test we want you to pay close attention to how hard you feel the exercise work rate is. This feeling should reflect your total amount of exertion and fatigue, combining all sensations and feelings of physical stress, effort and fatigue. Don't concern yourself with any one factor such as leg pain, shortness of breath or exercise intensity, but try to concentrate on your total inner feeling of exertion. Try not to underestimate or overestimate your feelings of exertion; be as accurate as you can.*

(Morgan et al., 1976)

For basic information about the scale construction, metric properties, correct administration etc., refer to *Borg's Perceived Exertion and Pain Scales* (Borg G, 1998, Human Kinetics).

By monitoring your training load effectively, via heart rate, GPS and the RPE scale, it should be possible to avoid over-training syndromes and illness.

## Over-training: immune system response to exercise

Moderate regular exercise has been shown to boost the immune system and reduce upper respiratory tract infections (URTIs). However, it has been shown that intense regular exercise can compromise the immune system since, during intense physical exertion, the body produces certain hormones that temporarily lower immunity.

Studies on the influence of moderate exercise training on host protection and immune function have shown that near daily brisk walking compared with inactivity reduced the number of sickness days by half over a 12- to 15-week period without a change in resting immune function (Nieman *et al.*, 1999). The same research indicates that too much intense exercise can reduce immunity, and that more than 90 minutes of high-intensity endurance exercise can make athletes susceptible to illness for up to 72 hours after the exercise session.

Nieman (1997) suggests that endurance athletes are at increased risk of URTIs during periods of heavy training and in the one- to two-week period after marathon-type race events. This is important information for those who compete in longer events.

Several researchers have reported a diminished neutrophil function in athletes during periods of intense and heavy training. Following each bout of prolonged heavy endurance exercise, several components of the immune system appear to demonstrate suppressed function for several hours. This has led to the concept of the 'open window', described as the three- to twelve-hour time period after prolonged endurance exercise, when host defence is decreased and the risk of URTI is elevated.

There is sufficient evidence for sports medicine professionals to encourage athletes to practise various hygiene measures to lower their risk of URTIs and to avoid heavy exertion during systemic illness.

Nieman *et al.* (1999) looked into the influence of nutritional supplementation that could potentially reduce the incidence of URTIs as a result of intense heavy training. The influence of nutritional supplements – primarily zinc, vitamin C, glutamine and carbohydrate – on the acute immune response to prolonged exercise has been measured in endurance athletes.

## UPPER RESPIRATORY TRACT INFECTIONS (URTIs)

URTIs are the illnesses caused by an acute infection that involves the upper respiratory tract, this being the nose, sinuses, larynx and pharynx. Such illnesses, like the common cold, sinusitis, sore throat, fever, nasal congestion, bronchitis and sneezing, are all URTIs. The onset of the symptoms usually begins one to three days after exposure to a microbial pathogen, most commonly a virus. The duration of the symptoms is typically seven to ten days, but may persist for longer.

*Neutrophils* are the most common type of white blood cell, comprising about 50–70 per cent of all white blood cells. They are phagocytic, which means that they can ingest other cells, though they do not survive the act. Neutrophils are the first immune cells to arrive at a site of infection, through a process known as chemotaxis.

Though neutrophils are short-lived, with a half-life of four to ten hours when not activated and immediate death upon ingesting a pathogen, they are plentiful, and responsible for the bulk of an immune response. Neutrophils are present in the bloodstream until signalled to a site of infection by chemical cues in the body. They are fast acting, arriving at the site of infection within an hour.

Vitamin C and glutamine have received much media attention, but the data thus far is inconclusive. However, the most impressive results to aid a positive immune response after intense exercise have been reported in carbohydrate supplementation studies. Carbohydrate beverage ingestion has been associated with a number of positive anti-inflammatory and immune responses in the body (Nieman *et al.*, 1999). Despite this, more research is needed to identify whether carbohydrate supplementation actually reduces the frequency of infections after strenuous exercise.

The main points to consider in order to reduce the incidence of infections after strenuous exercise are to:

- eat a healthy, well balanced diet;
- keep well hydrated;
- wash your hands with hot, soapy water on a regular basis;
- avoid people with colds and flu if at all possible;
- avoid putting your hands close to your eyes, mouth and nose;
- use a hand gel sanitiser;

- listen to your body – rest and recover when your body tells you to!

This strategy should reduce the incidence of URTIs during your intense training periods.

## How to avoid over-training

If Eskimos have lots of words for snow, sports scientists have lots of words for over-training. As we have discussed already, the key to making improvements in your performance is not only to undertake the correct type of training session, but also to allow your body adequate time to recover afterwards.

Constantly pushing your body too hard in training, or suddenly increasing either the intensity or volume, is certain to cause excessive fatigue, which will disrupt your training as you have to take extended periods of rest. This is what we call over-training – in mild cases it will just be a case of having a few days' rest to recover from a particularly hard period of training; in extreme cases, it can cause your immune system to be suppressed and leave you vulnerable to virus infections that may have long-term implications for your health. So it is important to be aware of the causes and symptoms of over-training.

Sudden increases in training intensity or training volume are to be avoided. But even if you increase your training gradually, there are other factors that may still lead to over-training. Too little sleep, stress at work or in your home life, or an undetected illness can all lead to over-training symptoms. There are a multitude of symptoms of over-training, the expression of which may vary depending upon the athlete's physical and physiological make-up, the type of exercise undertaken and other factors. The individual has to learn to listen to their body and learn from experience in order to correctly identify when these symptoms are a sign of over-training and when they're simply a normal level of fatigue after a hard training session. Keeping track of your resting pulse rate first thing in the morning is a good way of spotting signs of over-training.

There are six key physiological responses to training to be aware of. They will help you differentiate between what is a normal response to training and what may be the onset of over-training.

1 **Training overload:** the training stress itself.
2 **Training fatigue/stress:** normal fatigue associated with heavy training.
3 **Over-training:** where training causes the individual so much stress that they are unable to perform at an optimal level following an appropriate regeneration period; a drop in performance is also experienced.
4 **Over-reaching:** follows intentional or unintentional short-term over-training; symptoms can be reversed with a longer regeneration period.

5 **Over-training syndrome:** chronically depressed performance as well as other symptoms; significant rest is required.

6 **Over-strain:** follows acute muscle damage by isolated intensive training; may or may not be associated with over-reaching or over-training syndrome.

## Symptoms of over-training

The symptoms of over-training may fall into five different areas: physiological, performance-related, psychological, immunological and biochemical. An athlete may show signs of only one of these symptoms, or an array. Many sports scientists suggest that the athlete's own results, rather than comparison to a standard population, must be used to identify the subtle changes that may be indicative of the onset of over-training.

Generally, over-training syndrome is a form of chronic fatigue. In the elite athlete, there may be a fragile balance between peak performance and chronic fatigue. For these athletes, as much as six weeks of full rest can be necessary to return individuals to their normal state.

While Fry *et al.* (1991) list many symptoms of over-training, the most common are listed in table 4.1.

| **Table 4.1 Common over-training symptoms** | |
|---|---|
| **Performance indicators** | **Physiological indices** |
| • Abnormal muscle soreness or pain<br>• Heavy legged feeling<br>• General inability to undertake training<br>• Drop off in performance<br>• Reduced endurance capacity | • Increased resting heart rate<br>• Suppressed training heart rate (for a given intensity)<br>• Elevated post exercise heart rate<br>• Excessive thirst |
| **Health related signs** | **Psychological signs** |
| • Abnormal fluctuations in body weight<br>• Loss of appetite<br>• Increased nocturnal fluid intake<br>• General lower resistance (for example more sore throats, mouth ulcers, common colds)<br>• Poor healing of wounds<br>• Disturbed sleep<br>• Gastro-intestinal disturbances | • Increased night sweating<br>• Generalised apathy/lethargy<br>• Shortened attention span<br>• Irritability<br>• Impaired co-ordination<br>• General loss of interest in training<br>• Depression |

## Occurrence of over-training syndrome

If we reconsider the model of training overload (*see* Figure 2.3), we can see how over-training syndrome develops and occurs in three different phases:

- **Phase 1:** Following a hard training session, discomfort may be felt in the muscle, and perceived exertion while exercising may increase. This is essentially the regeneration phase from points B to C. This can soon be rectified with rest.
- **Phase 2:** If the athlete persists with training, before recovery has been achieved (point C), there will be a further decline in performance, and other symptoms may develop. A few days of rest may be sufficient to prevent the progression of the syndrome.
- **Phase 3:** If the athlete continues to train without adequate rest (thereby repeating phases 1 and 2), full-blown over-training syndrome may occur. Other external stresses (e.g. relating to the athlete's nutrition, environment, sleep or work) could stimulate this.

While the exact mechanism and underlying causes of over-training are not fully known, there are ways of avoiding it happening in the first place. The basic principles of training must be adhered to, as outlined below:

- Use heart rate to gauge training intensity.
- Use a training diary (to record diet, training, mood, and so on).

- Continually review training responses.
- Use an interesting and continually changing training programme.
- Undertake physiological and, where necessary, psychological assessment.
- Implement correct nutritional practices.
- Where possible, remove other external sources of stress.

## Treatment of over-training syndrome

In order to treat over-training, rest is key. It is vital to reduce or stop training and minimise the previously described risks. Once sufficient rest to recover from all the associated symptoms has been taken, training should recommence slowly and cautiously, with additional rest being taken in the early stages. The use of tapers may prove effective for the elite athlete, to ensure full recovery prior to major competitions.

# Using resting heart rate to identify over-training

Your heart rate monitor is not just a vital tool in monitoring the intensity of your training sessions. It can also be used to indicate early signs of over-training.

The best time to take your resting heart rate is first thing in the morning when you wake up. It is possible to take it at other times during the day, but it's easiest first thing in the morning, when you're at your most rested.

Taking your resting heart rate may seem like another chore to be added to an already demanding training regime, but it really is worth taking the time to do it. It is the best and easiest way of determining whether you have recovered sufficiently from your last race or hard training session, and it takes some of the guesswork out of assessing your fatigue level.

Illness will also suppress your immune function and elevate your heart rate. During this time, monitor your resting heart rate carefully. However, be warned that although your resting heart rate may return to its baseline, your immune function will remain suppressed for a

## HOW TO TAKE YOUR RESTING HEART RATE

Before you go to bed, set your alarm 15 minutes earlier than normal and have your heart rate monitor next to the bed. When your alarm sounds, roll over, put on your monitor strap and start recording your heart rate. Set your alarm to snooze for 15 minutes so you can effectively record your resting heart rate. Now lie back and relax for the full 15 minutes.

Once you have completed the 'snooze test', look at your heart rate monitor and check for the lowest average minute. This is your resting heart rate reading. If your heart rate monitor does not record your heart rate in this way, note down the average heart rate over the 15 minutes.

If you don't have a heart rate monitor, you can use your right index and middle fingers to measure your resting heart rate from either your carotid artery in your neck or your radial artery in your wrist. Do not use your thumb as there is a small pulse there as well, which may affect your measurement. Begin your count with 0 (zero), then continue. Either count the number of beats over 15 seconds and multiply this by 4 or count for one minute to get your beats per minute value.

Whatever method you use, make sure you stick to it each time you check your resting heart rate. You really need to check this at least once, and possibly twice, a week. Initially, it is best to do this the day after a rest day, when you are fully recovered. For example, if you trained on Sunday and Monday is your rest day, you need to do the test on the Tuesday morning, ideally 36–48 hours after your last training session.

Once you have this fully recovered heart rate reading, you can use it to highlight days when you are still fatigued. If you wake up not feeling 100 per cent, and your heart rate monitor gives a reading that is more than five beats above your normal baseline, this is an indication that you may need to take things easy, or maybe not train at all that day.

1 Lie down and rest comfortably for 10 minutes at the same time each day (morning is best).
2 At the end of 10 minutes, record your heart rate in beats per minute (or complete upon waking).
3 Stand up. While still standing:
  – after 15 seconds, take a second heart rate in beats per minute
  – after 90 seconds, take a third heart rate in beats per minute
  – after 120 seconds, take a fourth heart rate in beats per minute.

Well-rested athletes will show a consistent heart rate between measurements, but Rusko *et al.* found a marked increase (10 beats per minute or more) in the 120-second post-standing measurement of athletes on the verge of over-training.

Such a change may indicate that you have not recovered from a previous workout, are fatigued or otherwise stressed, and it may be helpful to reduce training or rest for another day before performing another workout or training session.

## MEASURING YOUR RESTING HEART RATE AND THE ORTHOSTATIC HEART RATE TEST

The measurement of resting heart rate (RHR) is a great indicator of how conditioned an individual's cardiovascular system is, and also an effective measure of over-training. Your heart rate is controlled by the nervous system, and this is one of the first three systems to show signs of over-training. Thus, nervous system irregularities show up as changes in heart rate, which you can monitor quite easily, without the need for expensive tests, so it becomes a very easy and useful tool during intense training and conditioning periods.

In general, the higher your RHR, the more deconditioned you are; the lower it is, the fitter you are. Some elite athletes have an RHR of under 40 bpm. Normal resting heart rate values for adults range from around 60–80 bpm. The fitter you are, the more efficient your cardiovascular system is, with a larger stroke volume and increased cardiac output, which means that oxygen gets to the muscles in the body more efficiently.

## A TRUE STORY: ANECDOTAL EVIDENCE OF OVER-TRAINING SYNDROME

*Wayne Keet, endurance athlete*

## Background

Four years of ultra-marathon running [in the Comrades Marathon] led to some swimming and cycling as part of my cross-training during injury. My type A personality did not allow any rest days. Actually, after the 2003 Comrades Marathon, I was back running two days later.

I started triathlon in 2003, and again went straight in at the deep end and entered Ironman Switzerland. So, after a very successful 2002, with no 'off-season', I jumped straight into training for 2003. My schedule seemed a little hectic to me, suicidal to friends.

A long-distance duathlon six days before the London Marathon didn't seem to affect my time as I managed to run 2 hours 59. I headed off to the Comrades Marathon on 16 June 2003 with Ironman Switzerland five weeks later.

After Switzerland, where, by now, my body started to feel a little 'jaded', I did the Half-Ironman UK three weeks later. So, when August came round, I was already toast. But as I had qualified for the World Championships in Queenstown, New Zealand, in December, I then started to smash the speed sessions for the shorter distance.

It came as no surprise that I had a shocker at the World Championships. I let myself down. Again, instead of heeding the warning signs of over-training/racing, I then arrived back in December 2003 and went off to South Africa, which was supposed to be three weeks of sun, sea and beer.

Lo and behold, I got caught up training with my friends and it turned into three weeks of the most intense training ever. Only because I was able to sleep four hours during the day was I able to do these sessions.

January 2004 rolled around, and I was trying to keep my eyes open. I was still managing to complete some solid run sessions, but I remember literally waking up halfway through a swim session at 6 am one morning.

Then, one morning when I awoke to run a 20-mile race, my glands were swollen, a definite sign that my body was pretty much broken. Still, no respite for me, off I went to run the race. Afterwards, I slept from 11 am until 8 am the next morning. And, even when I woke up, I felt like I had been hit by a bus.

The next two months were a constant battle between my fatigue and trying to get some results from doctors etc. Nothing showed up in blood tests, not even glandular fever. Eventually I had to stop work as I was not able to stay awake during the day.

I did the usual food intolerance testing, cutting out certain foods etc., but I was still no better. It was only when Dr Tim Noakes from the Sports Science Institute in Cape Town came to London to give a talk, that I managed to speak to someone. He put me in touch with a fellow sports doctor down at Portsmouth University who had been through the same condition, chronic fatigue syndrome/over-training, when trying for the Athens Olympics.

It was only after our first meeting that it dawned on me: the severity of how burned out I was.

I had to start keeping a diary on sleep, food and general feeling/well-being. At this stage, I was definitely in a state of depression. I refused to go on to antidepressants, as I swore to myself that I would get myself out of this mess 'naturally'.

By October 2004 I was allowed to walk for five minutes and increase that by two minutes every second day. The minute I felt tired, I had to stop. Self-discipline played a huge part here, as my previous tendency was to push through.

By February 2005 I was running 21 km again and was on the road to recovery. One year had been lost, but so many lessons learned.

Nowadays, I am more in tune with my body and can spot the first sign of reaching the cliff edge of over-training.

# 5
# RUNNING INJURIES

Unfortunately injuries are often experienced by those of us who choose to exercise and push ourselves physically, and running is no exception. Research indicates that chronic injuries are more common in runners than more acute injuries, which are more common in contact sports such as rugby and football. It may be possible to try to foresee and reduce the occurrence of injuries by using screening techniques.

## Screening

There are many ways that healthcare professionals, strength and conditioning coaches, exercise physiologists and chartered physiotherapists can screen an athlete before they begin an exercise programme. The PAR-Q is a questionnaire-based approach (*see* page 27), which provides useful information about the client. There are also more dynamic methods that may

complement such tools as the PAR-Q, as they assess the movement patterns of the participant, which may indicate a number of issues that need to be addressed or would potentially predispose the participant to injury.

In professional sports teams you may have a review with the sports medicine doctor and the physiotherapist. If you are a recreational athlete you may go and see your GP for a check-up and a chat about your history, and gain clearance if necessary. This is important in order to clear up any potential risk factors.

One effective way to screen is to evaluate specific movement patterns that may predispose an individual to injury. This is more than just a chat with your doctor or lying on a couch with a physiotherapist; this is a functional review and scoring assessment that, research has shown, will indicate your injury potential.

One such screen is the Functional Movement Screen (FMS)™. This is a tool that allows the assessor to evaluate the functional movement of an individual via seven different movement screens. It is used widely in professional sport and has been shown to correlate highly with injury potential based upon the score achieved. Specifically, the FMS is a ranking and grading system created to document movement patterns that are key to normal function. By screening these patterns, functional limitations and asymmetries are readily identified. Basic movement pattern limitations can reduce the effects of functional training and physical conditioning, and distort proprioception (body awareness). As a result of completing the FMS, each athlete will achieve a score that helps to target the problem and track progress. The scoring system is directly linked to the most beneficial corrective exercises to restore mechanically sound movement patterns.

The seven screens that need to be performed in order to complete the FMS are as follows:

1  Deep squat
2  Hurdle step
3  In-line lunge
4  Shoulder mobility
5  Active straight-leg raise
6  Trunk stability push-up
7  Rotational stability

The FMS should be introduced as part of the pre-participation physical examination, to determine deficits that may be overlooked during the traditional medical and performance evaluations.

In many cases during a normal screen (with an evaluation on a couch or based on a question-naire), muscle flexibility and strength imbalances, along with previous injuries, may not be identified. These problems, which have been acknowledged as significant risk factors for injury, will be identified using the FMS.

This dynamic assessment will pinpoint func-tional deficits related to proprioceptive, mobility and stability weaknesses. If these risk factors can be identified and addressed utilising the FMS, then decreases in injuries and improved performance should follow.

The FMS should be administered by accredited personnel to ensure the validity and reliability of the screening tests.

## Common running injuries

Despite best efforts with stretching, screening and application of best practice, as a result of the high-impact nature of running, injury can still occur. Knobloch *et al.* (2008) state that Achilles tendinopathy is the most common injury for runners. This is followed by anterior knee pain, shin splints and plantar fasciitis. The research indicates that, at some time, 56.6 per cent of athletes have had Achilles tendon over-use injury, 46.4 per cent anterior knee pain,

35.7 per cent shin splints and 12.7 per cent plantar fasciitis.

Taunton *et al.* (2002) analysed the running injuries at a primary care sports medicine facility. From their research, they found that patellofemoral pain syndrome (anterior knee pain) was the most common injury, followed by iliotibial band friction syndrome, plantar fasciitis, meniscal injuries of the knee, and tibial stress syndrome (shin splints).

Each study will identify different 'common' injuries, dependent upon the demographic of the sample group and the individuals involved: their age, gender, training history, injury history, height, weight, weekly load, etc. One thing that is highlighted through these studies is that lower limb injuries do occur to a significant number of runners, with the incidence varying from between 30 and 79 per cent (Buist *et al.*, 2007).

The top five most common injuries for runners, based on a review of the current research appear to be the following:

1 Achilles tendinopathy
2 Anterior knee pain (patellofemoral pain syndrome)
3 Tibial stress syndrome (shin splints)
4 Plantar fasciitis
5 Iliotibial band friction syndrome

Below we review each of these injuries, including its symptoms and what you should do if you experience any of these during your running career.

## Achilles tendinopathy

Achilles tendinopathy is a degenerative disorder of the Achilles tendon and not an inflammatory condition as previously thought. As such, non-steroidal anti-inflammatory drugs (NSAIDS) do not help this condition.

It is now widely recognised that the key to restoring normal function of the Achilles is to promote healing without overloading the tendon. In the early stages of the condition eccentric calf raises should form the main part of treatment (*see* Figure 5.1). During eccentric exercises pain is often felt; this is common and you should progress through it.

**Figure 5.1 Eccentric loading and prescription (do three sets of 15 twice a day). Start position.**

Typical symptoms of Achilles tendinopathy are stiffness of the Achilles first thing in the morning, and a pain that 'warms up' and feels better during exercise, but feels worse once the body has cooled down or on waking the next morning. The area may be mildly swollen, will be tender and may creak, either with movement or when touched (this is called crepitus). It is an over-use injury and will frequently result from increased running mileage, shoes with decreased impact protection or a change of running surface (e.g. from treadmill to road).

Rehabilitation must focus on loading the Achilles in a controlled way and then, over time, progressing the load applied to the tendon by increasing the number of repetitions of eccentric exercises and eventually progressively increasing running.

Ice, deep calf massage, stretching and deep friction to the Achilles will help to relieve symptoms and should form part of the treatment following loading the tendon.

Depending on how long you have had the symptoms the recovery can be slow. For long-standing Achilles tendinopathy, even after starting the correct treatment recovery can take three months for full recovery. However, if you notice there is very little recovery with these exercises you should consult a sports physician as there are injections and, in some cases, surgical options available.

**Figure 5.1 (cont.) Concentric preparation (top) and single leg eccentric loading (bottom).**

## Anterior knee pain (patellofemoral pain syndrome)

With patellofemoral pain the main aim of treatment is to restore normal alignment of the patella in relation to the femur. The earlier this can be done the better, to avoid permanent damage to the articular surfaces.

The typical symptoms of patellofemoral pain include pain and stiffness after long periods sitting in limited space (sometimes called the 'cinema' sign), pain worse going downstairs (or downhill) than upstairs, and creaking of the knees. Quite often a squat is painful at the start of the range, but it is possible to 'go through' this and find that once fully squatting on the haunches the knee is pain free. The knee does not typically swell dramatically, but sometimes patients will notice a 'puffiness' or low grade swelling at the front of the knee.

It is best to have a review with a chartered physiotherapist to assess your individual problem as it can be caused by a number of different biomechanical reasons (*see* Figure 5.2).

Commonly, iliotibial band (ITB) tightness and vastus medialis (VMO) weakness cause the patella to track laterally and this, in turn, causes pain. In this instance, ITB stretching as well as vastus medialis strengthening is indicated. VMO can be targeted by externally rotating the feet while performing quad-strengthening exercises.

Depending on how your patella tracks against the femur there are various taping or bracing strategies that can be used to encourage correct alignment. Your physiotherapist may also need to mobilise the patella with manual techniques to restore normal function.

## Tibial stress syndrome (shin splints)

Treatment for tibial stress syndrome (*see* Figure 5.3) includes identifying the cause and addressing this issue, as it is primarily a biomechanical problem.

The symptoms of medial tibial stress syndrome are felt along the bony inner border of the shin. The area can ache after impact exercise and is locally tender. Increasing tenderness and pain focused around one point, typically at the

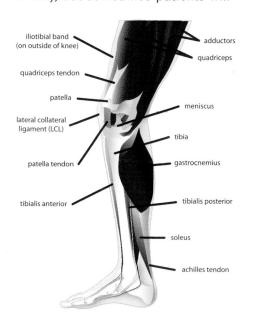

iliotibial band (on outside of knee)
adductors
quadriceps
quadriceps tendon
patella
meniscus
lateral collateral ligament (LCL)
tibia
patella tendon
gastrocnemius
tibialis anterior
tibialis posterior
soleus
achilles tendon

**Figure 5.2 Knee musculature and ligaments/structures**

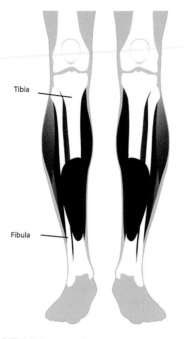

Tibia

Fibula

**Figure 5.3 Tibial stress syndrome**

will overload the muscles in the shin as well as elsewhere in the body.

A chartered physiotherapist will help by performing deep-tissue work on the muscles that become irritated and inflamed. Joints and muscles above the injury must also be looked at. Iliotibial band (ITB) stretching may be required if tightness in this area is affecting running mechanics.

Prevention is best accomplished with smart training. Make sure you have days that are low-impact (e.g. cycling or swimming) with no running.

junction of the lower third and upper two-thirds of the shin bone, may indicate the presence of a stress fracture and should be reviewed by a sports physician.

Most commonly, people who overpronate the foot while walking or running apply increased amounts of stress to the muscles on the front of the shin. This results in an over-use injury and severe pain on the anterior shin, causing 'shin splints'.

First, the biomechanical issue must be addressed, and suitable footwear that supports the foot and prevents abnormalities must be worn. You must also look at your training regime. If you are running too far too soon you

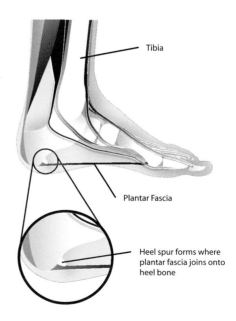

Tibia

Plantar Fascia

Heel spur forms where plantar fascia joins onto heel bone

**Figure 5.4 Plantar fascia**

## Plantar fasciitis

The pain of plantar fasciitis is felt under the heel bone (calcaneum), where the fascia attaches (see Figure 5.4); it then runs forward, 'bowstringing' under the medial (inner) arch of the foot and supporting it.

It is an over-use injury, often caused by an increase in impact activity, or by wearing shoes that are too thin-soled or that inadequately support the foot arch. A tight calf will also increase pressure on the plantar fascia. Sometimes it can be associated with a sharp, bony spur forming at its attachment to the calcaneum, causing mechanical pressure on the fascia. However, more commonly it results from soft tissue inflammation and is felt constantly in one place, with all weight-bearing activity, particularly if the heel is not cushioned by footwear.

Initial treatment options include the following.

- Stretching exercises: exercises that stretch out the calf muscles help ease pain and assist with recovery.
- Deep friction can be applied to the calcaneus (normally the main point of pain in plantar fasciitis).
- Avoid going barefoot: when you walk without shoes, you put undue strain and stress on your plantar fascia.
- Ice: putting your foot into a bucket of iced water for up to 20 minutes several times a day will help reduce inflammation.
- Limit/reduce activities.
- Shoe modifications: wearing supportive shoes that have good arch support and a slightly raised heel reduces stress on the plantar fascia. Your shoes should provide a comfortable environment for the foot.
- Medications: NSAIDs, such as ibuprofen, may help reduce pain and inflammation.
- Lose weight: extra pounds put extra stress on your plantar fascia.

If you still have pain after several weeks it is likely that you will need further intervention; you should see your doctor or chartered physiotherapist, who may add one or more of the following approaches.

- Padding and strapping: placing pads in the shoe softens the impact of walking; strapping helps support the foot and reduce strain on the fascia.
- Orthotic devices that fit into your shoe help correct the underlying structural abnormalities causing the plantar fasciitis.
- Injection therapy: in some cases, corticosteroid injections are used to help reduce the inflammation and relieve pain.
- Removable walking cast: a removable walking cast may be used to keep your foot immobile for a few weeks, to allow it to rest and heal.
- Night splint: wearing a night splint allows you to maintain an extended stretch of the plantar fascia while sleeping; this may help reduce the morning pain experienced by some patients.
- Physical therapy: exercises and other physical therapy measures may be used to help provide relief.

Although most patients with plantar fasciitis respond to non-surgical treatment, a small percentage of patients may require surgery. If, after several months of non-surgical treatment, you continue to have heel pain, surgery will be considered.

## Iliotibial band friction syndrome

The iliotibial band (ITB) (*see* Figure 5.5) is an area that is often neglected by athletes, particularly runners. They know they must stretch the quads and calf muscles but often don't even know about the ITB until it is too late and an over-use injury has occurred. The ITB should be stretched as a part of a runner's general stretching programme.

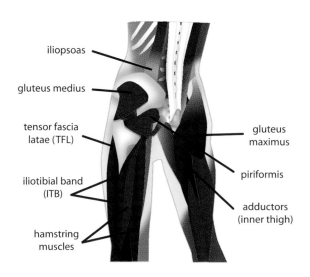

iliopsoas

gluteus medius

tensor fascia
latae (TFL)

iliotibial band
(ITB)

hamstring
muscles

gluteus
maximus

piriformis

adductors
(inner thigh)

**Figure 5.5 The iliotibial band (ITB) shown in relation to the muscles of the lower back, hip and thigh.**

The ITB causes problems when it gets so tight that it starts to rub against the natural bony prominences of the outside of the leg, causing friction, inflammation and therefore pain. It can catch either at the top part of the tibia, to the side of the knee, or over the greater trochanter of the femur, to the side of the hip. Pain will worsen with increased mileage, but may 'warm up' so that symptoms are worst after running or even the next day. Tenderness over the bony prominence itself will be present, as well as a sharper pain with movement when the ITB catches on the area. In some cases a click can be heard as the ITB rubs on the bone, but this is not common.

If you do develop ITB friction syndrome, treatment begins with the biomechanical issues, including a footwear review and specific stretches. Limiting excessive training, resting for a period of time, and incorporating low-impact cross-training activities will also help. A physiotherapist will perform deep-tissue release of the ITB and connecting tensor fascia lata, and help with stretching. NSAIDs may be prescribed by your doctor to help decrease the inflammatory response around the area of irritation.

These treatments should always be attempted first. However, if they fail to offer improvement, an injection of cortisone into the area of inflammation may also be attempted. If all else fails, surgery is an option, but only in very rare circumstances.

## Foot care

Foot care is an essential part of injury prevention and cannot be underestimated by any athlete, especially runners. In addition to the above information on chronic injuries, you should also be aware of the following important points on foot care and running shoe selection.

## TOP TIPS FOR RUNNING SHOE SELECTION

- Buy a sport-specific shoe – avoid cross-trainers when running.
- Go shoe shopping later in the day when your feet are at their largest.
- Take the socks you will be wearing with you.
- Get the assistant to measure your feet when you are standing up, as the foot elongates on weight bearing.
- The shoe should be 1 cm longer than your longest toe when you have fastened the shoe and you are standing up – 90 per cent of people wear the wrong-sized shoes.
- Avoid slip-on shoes as, by design, these have to be too tight to stay on.
- Avoid stitching or design work over prominent joints or toes, to avoid irritation.
- If you have corns or calluses on the joints of your toes, or you regularly lose toenails when running, your shoes are too small/shallow.
- Do not wash your trainers in the washing machine; it will damage the sole materials and impair their function.
- If the correct sized shoe does not feel comfortable, pick a different style not a different size.
- Change your trainers every 500 miles to avoid injury.
- Avoid flat shoes as these place undue stress through the calf muscle complex and mid-foot area.
- A good trainer should flex only where the toes bend, not in the mid-foot area, which should be stable.
- You should not be able to twist the shoe.
- Manufacturers design trainers with variable eyelets so you can fine-tune the fit:
  - narrow foot – use the eyelets that are set wider
  - wide foot – use the eyelets that are found closer to the tongue
  - foot pain – if you have a bony prominence on the top of the foot, leave a space in the lacing to alleviate pressure
  - high-arch foot – avoid criss-cross lacing, which increases the pressure down the centre of the tongue
  - slipping heel – secure the top of the shoe to stop the heel slipping; lace normally until

you reach the second to last eyelet, then make a vertical loop on each side; thread the loose laces through the opposite loops to pull the sides of the shoe in more firmly.

- Several manufacturers make trainers in two width fittings: narrow and wide.
- It is a myth that orthotics wearers should purchase neutral trainers; an orthotic works best on a stable surface that it cannot sink into.
- When looking for a running shoe, get an expert to assess your foot type or watch you run and give you appropriate advice on styles to try.

## A BASIC GUIDE TO RUNNING SHOES

- Neutral shoes are for supinated (stiff, highly arched) foot types. They offer minimal support, but maximum cushioning.
- Stability shoes are for moderate overpronators (average arch height). They offer good support and cushioning, and are suitable for the majority of runners.
- Motion-control shoes are for extreme overpronators (mobile foot type, lower arch profile). They provide excellent support but are heavier shoes.
- If you are a bigger build, you may have to go for a more stable shoe than your foot type dictates, to get the support you require when running.

Additional research by Buist *et al.* (2008) indicates that those with no prior running experience were more susceptible to running-related injuries, and that males were more susceptible than females. This highlights that the new runner needs to be very gradual in their approach and their progressive overload of training, in addition to having the right equipment. By being more gradual, the body will adapt more effectively and injury potential will be reduced.

## PROGRESSIVE OVERLOAD

**All well designed training programmes incorporate the concept of progressive overload.**

This principal holds that to maximise the benefits of training, the training stimulus must be progressively increased as the body adapts to the current stimulus. Your body responds to training by adapting to the stress of the training stimulus. If the amount of stress remains constant, you will eventually adapt fully to that level of stimulation and your body won't need further adaptation. The only way to continue to improve with training is to progressively increase the training stimulus or stress.

Source: Wilmore and Costill, 1994

Macera (1992) states that previous injury history has a strong effect on future injury potential. Among the risk factors studied, weekly distance is the strongest predictor of future injuries. Other training characteristics (speed, frequency, surface and timing) have little or no effect on future injuries after accounting for distance.

Macera gives the following advice for runners who have experienced previous injury:

- For recreational runners who have sustained injuries, especially within the past year, a reduction in running to below 32 km per week is recommended.
- For those about to begin a running programme, moderation is the best advice.
- For competitive runners, great care should be taken to ensure that prior injuries are sufficiently healed before attempting any racing event, particularly a marathon.

## Blisters

Another problem, not yet mentioned but experienced by most athletes at one time or another, is blisters. And they can be debilitating! Even professional athletes like Novak Djokovich experience blisters. Djokovich apparently withdrew from the Wimbledon Championships Semi-Final in 2007 against Raphael Nadal because of an infected blister.

How many times have you arrived at an event and seen some of your running colleagues about to start the race with their brand new, sparkling running shoes on, fresh out of the box? They may look good, but it spells trouble! Blisters are a simple yet common problem with athletes wearing–in new shoes, as well as runners or walkers who take part in exceptionally long events such as marathons or long hill walks. They are usually caused by friction of some kind, a kink in any foot tape, socks or new shoes.

A blister is formed when fluid from blood vessels leaks into the skin. It then collects beneath the outer layer of skin, forming the typical raised pod, or 'blister'. As new skin grows beneath the blister, the fluid contained within it is slowly absorbed into the body and the skin on top dries and peels off. A blister will generally heal naturally without any treatment.

You should never burst a blister to release the fluid, however tempting it is. This is because the skin acts as a barrier against infection. When the skin of the blister breaks of its own accord, or as a result of minor trauma (like going for a run), cover it with a sterile, dry dressing to protect the area from infection until it has healed.

If the blister becomes red, hot, filled with pus or painful, then seek medical advice because you may need treatment for possible infection.

The good news is that blisters can usually be prevented by following the guidelines listed below:

- Ensure that shoes fit correctly.
- Protect potential 'hot spots' by applying a second skin and/or plasters or tape.

- Keep feet as dry as possible. Wet running shoes and socks will cause blisters far quicker than dry ones.
- Wherever possible, change socks regularly.
- Ensure that you don't save your brand new running shoes for the big event; wear in new running shoes gradually for good comfort and fit.

## Fungal infections

Another problem when you are running on a regular basis and don't give your feet a rest, is fungal infections.

There are many different types of fungi, and fungal infections of the feet are common. Foot infection normally starts in the toe web area, often spreading to the soles and toenails. Fungi thrive in warm, dark and moist conditions (i.e. sporty people who wear trainers!).

Infection is acquired by contact with skin debris carrying fungal elements. Signs and symptoms include itching, redness, scaling skin and blisters/vesicles. When the nails are infected, they become thickened, friable and discoloured.

## FOOT CARE TIPS

### Prevention

- Air the feet daily.
- Allow shoes to dry out for 24 hours before wearing them again.
- Avoid foot powders – they absorb moisture and provide the perfect environment for bacteria and fungi to multiply.
- Spray surgical spirit on the soles of the feet and between the toes daily to decrease perspiration.
- Wear flip-flops in communal areas.
- Wear cotton socks and leather shoes – avoid man-made materials.
- Maintain good hygiene.
- Wash feet in lukewarm water and dry well, especially between the toes.
- Do not share footwear.

### Treatment

- Skin and/or nail samples should be taken and sent for laboratory analysis to identify the infecting organism and determine the most appropriate treatment.
- Dry infections of the skin respond best to anti-fungal creams.
- Moist infections of the skin respond best to astringent anti-fungal sprays.

- Fungal infection of the nail plate is harder to eradicate, anti-fungal nail paint or a course of tablets is required.
- Shoes should be treated with anti-fungal sprays to prevent re-infection and the preventative measures discussed above should be employed long term.

## PRICE

As we have discovered, injury will occur in the majority of runners (between 30 and 79 per cent). The likelihood therefore is that, if you run, then you may well experience an injury. The injuries discussed above are generally chronic – meaning that they have occurred over time or are due to over-use. What about if you go for a run and suddenly experience pain, then what should you do? It is worth knowing that there are very effective basic first-aid guidelines that any athlete can adhere to in order to help treat and reduce the recovery time and severity of an acute injury.

Proper care up to 72 hours after injury can significantly reduce the time you're sidelined.

Should you suffer a sprain, strain, pull, tear or other muscle or joint injury, treat it with the RICE principle – Rest, Ice, Compression and Elevation – as soon as possible. More recently, the acronym has been increased to PRICE, with P representing 'Protection'.

PRICE can relieve pain, limit swelling and protect the injured tissue, all of which help to speed up healing. After an injury occurs, the damaged area will bleed (externally or internally) and become inflamed and swollen. By following the guidelines below you will reduce swelling and encourage healing, which will help towards a quicker recovery.

## THE PRICE PRINCIPLE: ACUTE INJURIES

- **Protection** Protection is required to protect the injured tissue from stress and movement which may disrupt the healing process. Weak bonds form in the tissues very soon after an injury and if these bonds are stressed too much they can break very easily, which then leads to re-inflammation, bleeding and swelling, and a general slowing-down of the healing process. This ultimately leads to a delay in the healing process rather than the desired effect of promoting healing. Protection may be applied in many different ways according to what you may have available – for example, taping the injured area may help (and will also compress the area), or the use of slings with an upper body injury and crutches for a lower body injury will all go towards protecting the injured area. By protecting or immobilising the area, you can help with pain relief and the healing process.

- **Rest** Rest is vital to protect the injured muscle, tendon, ligament or other tissue from further injury (keep off it!). In addition, your body needs to rest so it has the energy it needs to heal itself most effectively.
- **Ice** Use ice bags, cold packs or even a bag of frozen peas to cool the affected area. Wrap the ice bag or frozen peas in a thin tea towel to provide cold to the injured area. Cold can provide short-term pain relief (it is an analgesic). It also limits swelling by reducing blood flow to the injured area, which helps maintain a joint's range of movement (ROM) with injury. (**Caution:** You should never leave ice on an injury for more than 15–20 minutes at a time. Longer exposure can damage your skin. The best rule is to apply cold compresses for 15–20 minutes and then leave them off for at least 20 minutes to allow blood to flow back into the area, which aids healing.)
- **Compression** Compression limits swelling to the damaged area. Swelling will slow down healing time, so the compression will help the injured tissue recover and heal in the long run. Compression can also help with pain relief. If you have an elastic bandage (tubi-grip) or crepe bandage, then you can compress the area with that. If the area becomes more painful, the compression feels too tight or begins to throb, then loosen the compress.
- **Elevation** Elevating an injury also reduces swelling and is most effective when the injured area is raised above the level of the heart. For example, if you injure an ankle, try lying on your bed with your foot propped up on one or two pillows.

Source: adapted from Chartered Society of Physiotherapy, 1998

By responding to an injury with the PRICE principle you will be able to relieve pain, limit swelling and protect the injured tissue, all of which will help to speed up healing. However, if your pain or swelling hasn't reduced after 48 hours you should book an appointment to see your physician or a chartered physiotherapist, or go to A&E for a review and thorough diagnosis.

## Ice or heat?

Many people ask about heat for the treatment of injuries. Heat should never be used on acute injuries as it will encourage vasodilatation of the blood vessels and capillaries, which will encourage more fluid to the injured area. As you can see from the PRICE principle for acute injuries, one of the main targets with this method is a reduction in swelling, so heat would be a contraindication to this idea.

The same is true if you choose to have a hot bath after intense activity or unaccustomed exercise. It may be quite appealing to have a hot bath to 'relax the muscles', but the heat of a hot bath may well cause more trouble and reduce recovery time. You may have micro-tears in the muscle fibres after intense activity and, by heating the area, and with the physiological affect of vasodilatation, you will effectively make the muscles 'bleed', causing more stiffness. After a game of golf or low-impact exercise, a warm bath is probably OK, but it is probably best to leave it if you have just run your first 10 km or marathon!

There are, however, rationales for using heat post-exercise – for example, in contrast bathing (a recovery technique, discussed in chapter 6), but generally after a hard, intense training session it is best avoided.

Heat treatments should be used for chronic conditions only, to help relax and loosen tissues, and to stimulate blood flow to the area. Do not use heat treatments after activity, and do not use heat after an acute injury. Ice can be used with chronic injuries, but always after exercise to reduce the inflammatory response, never before exercise.

Heating tissues can be accomplished using a heating pad, hot water bottle or a hot, wet towel, but always make sure that you are very careful to use a moderate heat for a limited time, to avoid burning.

**Table 5.1 Quick reference guide to when to use heat and when to use ice**

|  | Ice treatment | Heat treatment |
| --- | --- | --- |
| **When to use it** | Acute injuries (muscular tears, sprains and strains, bruising and contusions) After activity for chronic injuries – for example, shin splints | Use heat before activities with chronic injuries, such as a sore Achilles Heat can help loosen tissues and relax injured areas after 48–72 hours (if acute) |
| **Duration of treatment** | Apply for between 15 and 20 minutes Leave off for 15–20 minutes and repeat for 2–3 cycles | Apply for no longer than 20 minutes at a time |

|  | Ice treatment | Heat treatment |
|---|---|---|
| How to apply treatment | Can be administered via cold packs, ice bags or frozen peas<br>Also put water in a cardboard cup and freeze; tear off the top of the cup for ice massage | A hot water bottle and hot, wet towels are both excellent methods |
| Cautions | Beware of ice burns | Beware of heat burns |

## Rehabilitation of your injury: practical guidelines

The first thing to do when you get injured is to evaluate the severity of the injury. Is it a case of PRICE for a few days, or should you see your physician or a chartered physiotherapist? If you are unsure, you should always seek professional medical advice.

Once you have determined the nature and severity of your injury it is time to think about your rehabilitation. If you purely rest and do nothing for a few weeks, you will de-train and have to re-start your conditioning programme from the beginning, which is demotivating and not ideal after all the hard work and effort you will already have put into your training programme. With just about every injury, there is always something you can do to maintain your fitness and conditioning.

The symptoms and treatment of chronic running injuries have been addressed above, so below are a few examples of common acute injuries for runners, and practical guidelines on how to go about your rehabilitation.

### Hamstring injury

Hamstring strains are among the most common injuries (and re-injuries) in athletes (Clanton and Coupe, 1998). The protocol of PRICE is the preferred initial treatment of hamstring injuries and you should proceed with this as soon as possible after injury.

As soon as the athlete is able to move without pain and walk without a limp, they should proceed with the accelerated running programme, adapted for use from Bruckner and Khan (2001).

The protocol shown in the box below should be followed by anyone who experiences a hamstring tear, with the most crucial element being to *listen to your body*. If at any time you feel pain or discomfort, you should stop and ice the injured area. This is an accelerated programme, as its name implies and, as a result, if you don't follow the guidelines carefully and strictly, you may re-injure yourself. If the programme is followed fully, however, it can be a great success.

If you have completed some fitness testing prior to your hamstring injury and you happened to complete some speed testing, specifically over 20 m, then it will provide you with some baseline data that will be extremely helpful during your hamstring rehabilitation (although this is not essential for the success of the rehab programme). If you have recorded your baseline 20 m speed then you will be able to effectively calculate the percentage speed over 20 m, which will help you evaluate how far along you may be in terms of reaching 'full fitness'. Calculate your 20 m speed at 70 per cent, 80 per cent and 90 per cent of your 20 m peak speed, so that when you progress your rehab you will be aware of how hard you are working and how close to your original 20 m peak speed you are getting. This is very important when you consider a return to full activity and the potential for re-injury.

For a runner, the accelerated hamstring programme itself will be challenging and sufficient to ensure a prompt and safe return to activity, training and, ultimately, competition. However, if you want to add some running drills to the specific protocol below, you could include some speed and agility work near to the end of the protocol. It is an acceleration–deceleration programme, so challenges straight-line running sufficiently, as required for runners from a hamstring point of view. It is easy enough to top up the protocol based on your own requirements, if necessary.

## ACCELERATED HAMSTRING PROGRAMME

### Phase 1
Target: 80 m runs x 6 (480 m). Complete three sets without any pain (total distance covered = 1440 m). Pace doesn't matter initially, volume is key.
Progress pace/speed of 80 m runs until about 70–80 per cent normal pace. This may take 3–4+ sessions repeating the same protocol.

### Phase 2: Accelerated running programme
The constant speed should be performed at around 70–75 per cent of the athlete's previously recorded peak speed time, if available from testing. The athlete will then continue and complete the following progressions in the same session:

| Acceleration | Constant speed | Deceleration | Repetitions | Distance covered |
|---|---|---|---|---|
| 40 m | | 40 m | | 100 m |
| 35 m | | 35 m | | 90 m |
| 30 m | 20 m | 30 m | x 2 of each | 80 m |
| 25 m | | 25 m | | 70 m |
| 20 m | | 20 m | | 60 m |
| 15 m | | 15 m | | 50 m |

Total distance covered = 900 m.
Rest = 15–20 seconds between repetitions.
Target: Complete two full sets; 2–3 minutes rest in between each set
(1800 m total distance).

**Phase 3: Progress accelerated running programme**
The constant speed should be performed at around 90 per cent of the athlete's previously recorded peak speed time, if available from testing.

| Acceleration | Constant speed | Deceleration | Repetitions | Distance covered |
|---|---|---|---|---|
| 40 m | | 40 m | | 100 m |
| 35 m | | 35 m | | 90 m |
| 30 m | | 30 m | | 80 m |
| 25 m | 20 m | 25 m | x 2 of each | 70 m |
| 20 m | | 20 m | | 60 m |
| 15 m | | 15 m | | 50 m |
| 10 m | | 10 m | | 40 m |
| 5 m | | 5 m | | 30 m |

Total distance covered = 1040 m.
Rest = 15–20 seconds between repetitions.
Target: Complete two full sets; 2–3 minutes rest in between each set (2080 m total distance).

**Phase 4: Optional depending upon specific requirements**

Multi-directional, agility and speed work, progress functional movement patterns and intensity.

If at any time the athlete experiences discomfort during the protocol they should immediately stop and ice.

There are no shortcuts to the protocol: all phases need to be completed pain free in order to progress to the next phase.

Source: adapted from Bruckner and Khan, 2001

In addition to the accelerated running programme, you could also add in some strengthening exercises. For more detail on strengthening exercises see chapter 7.

Of particular relevance to hamstring injuries and their prevention is the introduction of eccentric load.

## ECCENTRIC LOAD

Generally, muscles are known to create force when they contract (shorten) – for example, the movement from extension to flexion in order to complete a hamstring curl. This is known as concentric load (*see* Figure 5.6).

Eccentric load occurs when there is force placed upon the muscle while lengthening. An example of eccentric load, again using the hamstrings, would be extending the lower leg slowly from flexion to extension while a force is placed upon the limb. This movement can occur while prone – for example, while on a leg-curl machine where you would slowly lower your limb from a flexed position to an extended position. Eccentric work can also be completed in other positions. Another good example, and a great way to strengthen the hamstrings, is via Nordic curls, a straight-leg dead lift or a 'Good Morning' exercise (*see* Figure 5.7).

Figure 5.6 Hamstring curl indicating concentric load

A 'Good Morning' is where the athlete, in standing, would soften their knees and, tilting from the hips, slowly lower towards the floor maintaining a neutral spine. The back should always be 'flat' and protected, with the core turned on – little, if any weight is needed to overload the hamstring muscles.

**Figure 5.7 'Good Morning' exercise showing eccentric load**

## Ankle sprain

Another common lower-limb acute injury is an ankle sprain. Those of you who have experienced this will know how painful it is! A minor sprain is when a ligament is stretched or partially torn. In severe sprains, the ligament is completely torn. Sometimes the end of the bone to which a ligament is attached can crack and pull off, which is called an avulsion fracture. Ankle anatomy is shown in Figure 5.8.

As with every acute injury, as soon as possible, you should administer the PRICE principle. And, as with any injury, if you are in severe pain you should seek professional medical advice and diagnosis. The most common type of ankle sprain is when your foot turns inwards, overstretching the ligaments on the outside of your ankle. This is called an inversion sprain.

It has been demonstrated in a number of studies on ankle sprains and ankle injuries that it will generally take at least six weeks to three months before ligament healing occurs. However, at six weeks to one year after injury, a large percentage of participants still had

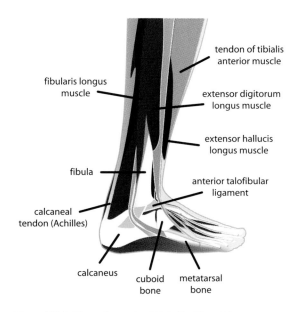

**Figure 5.8 Ankle anatomy showing ankle ligaments**

objective mechanical laxity and subjective ankle instability (Hubbard and Hicks-Little, 2008). This is why the rehabilitation of an injured ankle is so important. If you fail to rehabilitate your ankle sprain effectively then you are more likely to re-injure it and have ongoing problems.

As mentioned above, if your sprain is severe it may be advisable to see your physician or a chartered physiotherapist. They will assess the injury, may see you on a regular basis to treat the injury via manual therapy, and also possibly strap it with a 'horseshoe' pad to encourage the swelling to dissipate from the joint (see Figure 5.9). They may also recommend that you invest in a rigid support, like an Air Cast Stirrup® or even supply you with crutches.

Once the injury is beginning to settle, and you are beginning to weight-bear again, you can gradually begin your rehabilitation. As mentioned before, you can continue your conditioning with most injuries and an ankle sprain is no exception. Alternative modes of exercise include a stationary bike, arm ergometer and pool work. Always be guided by the pain: if it is painful, then stop.

As stated in the 'P' for Protection part of the PRICE principle, weak bonds form in the tissues very soon after an injury. If these bonds are stressed too much they can break very easily, which then leads to re-inflammation, bleeding and swelling, and a general slowing-down of the healing process. So, protect your injury and don't risk tearing these tissues as this is the beginning of the healing process.

Once weight-bearing is possible, then the main thing for any previously injured person to work on is regaining their normal gait pattern. If you have a limp and don't correct this early on, then you may experience secondary problems, like a sore knee, hip or lower back pain, as a result of poor movement patterns and compensation from other areas of the body.

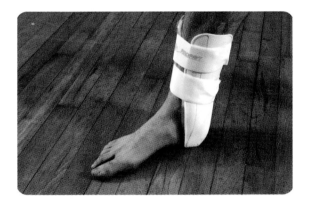

**Figure 5.9 Air Cast Stirrup® and horseshoe pad and tape**

Simple things like finding a local football pitch (with a good, even surface!) and walking along the white lines in your running shoes, with good form and a heel–toe strike, progressing to ensure that you have no limp or difference from the injured to non-injured side, is a simple and effective way to improve from an injured movement to an uninjured, 'normal' gait pattern.

As you get confident and stronger, you can progress the walk to push off more on your toes with large strides; then vary this with really small movements of heel–toe, heel–toe right next to each other, as if you are measuring how many feet a distance is.

There will be plenty of bruising generally with an ankle sprain, and ensuring that this moves and drains out of the area effectively is also important, otherwise the ankle can get 'clogged'. You can achieve this by pumping the ankle gently up and down, keeping it moving (within the limits of the pain), keeping it compressed, using a horseshoe pad and strapping and keeping it elevated as much as possible, especially early on. You can also use more hands-on techniques like massage.

Massage with arnica or an anti-inflammatory gel, like Ibuleve™ or Movelat™, for example, will help bring out the bruising and aid recovery, as well as encourage the swelling to be reabsorbed into the body and dissipate, which helps the ankle regain its ROM. Regaining the ankle's ROM is essential in the recovery process and to ensure that the gait pattern with walking, and ultimately running, is back to normal.

Proprioception (*see* box) is another essential component to reinstate and re-educate after an injury, and especially a joint injury like an ankle, shoulder or knee injury.

## PROPRIOCEPTION

Proprioception refers to the body's ability to sense movement within joints and joint positions.

This ability enables us to know where our limbs are in space without having to look. It is important in all everyday movements, but especially so in complicated sporting movements, where precise co-ordination is essential.

The proprioceptive system is made up of receptor nerves that are positioned in the muscles, joints and ligaments around the joints. These receptors can sense tension and stretch, and pass this information to the brain, where it is processed. The brain then responds by signalling to muscles to contract or relax in order to produce the desired movement. This system is subconscious; we don't have to think about it for it to work.

Following injury to joints and ligaments these receptors are damaged, which means the information that is usually sent to the brain is impaired. As a consequence the joint doesn't feel quite right and, in the long term, may be at risk of re-injury if these receptors aren't 're-trained' to work effectively again.

You don't need fancy equipment in order to complete proprioceptive work. Simple things like standing on one leg while cleaning your teeth, waiting in line or waiting for the bus will all re-train your ankle proprioceptors. You can also stand on a normal sofa cushion or pillow to make the surface a little bit more unstable, or progress by swinging the other leg or closing your eyes!

Always try to challenge yourself with proprioception exercises, as this work is very important.

It is also important to strengthen your ankle ligaments, which you can do via the use of special elastic bands (*see* Figure 5.10). You can get these bands (for example, Theraband™) from your local chemist or your local chartered physiotherapist. These exercises are, again, simple to do, and you can fit them into your daily routine – while sitting watching TV in the evening, for example.

**Figure 5.10 Band work: eversion, inversion start position, inversion (clockwise from above)**

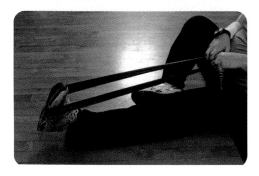

Figure 5.10 (cont.) Start position, plantar flexion, dorsi flexion

Once you can walk and complete some low-level proprioceptive training and band strengthening work then you should be at the point where you can begin to run again. The guideline that many chartered physiotherapists use to determine whether an athlete is ready to run is if they can

hop pain free. If you can complete five to ten pain-free hops in a row on your injured limb, then you should be able to cope with low-level running and be able to progress safely.

You may start with the following protocol (*see* table 5.2), but note that every injury and individual is different, and this protocol is purely a guide. You should always seek professional advice from a strength and conditioning coach or medical professional.

Although this plan may seem quite slow and precise, remember you can accelerate it if you feel good and are having no problems. You can also complement it with additional modes of exercise, like pool work, bike sessions and strength work, as well as your ongoing proprioception work, to help maintain your fitness and overall level of conditioning.

Once you start to build up the volume of running you are doing, then you can begin to increase the intensity and the speed back to where you used to be. As running is generally in one direction on a stable surface (unless you are a cross-country or fell runner) then you wouldn't necessarily need to complete the normal high-level end-stage rehabilitation of jumping, multi-directional movements and more challenging plyometrics, as much as a team sports player may do before you classify yourself as 'fit'.

However, it would make sense to complete some bounding and other running drills, so use

**Table 5.2 Example protocol for beginning to run again, post-injury**

| Work | Rest | Sets and repetitions | Total duration running |
|------|------|----------------------|------------------------|
| 1-minute run | 1-minute walk | 1 x 5 | 5 minutes |
| 2-minute run | 1-minute walk | 1 x 6 | 12 minutes |
| 2-, 4-, 6-minute run | 1-minute walk in between | 1 x set | 12 minutes |
| 6-minute runs | 1-minute walk in between each | 2 x sets | 12 minutes |
| 5-minute runs | 1-minute walk in between each | 3 x sets | 15 minutes |
| 2-, 4-, 6-, 8-minute run | 1-minute walk in between each | 1 x set | 20 minutes |
| 10-minute run | 2-minute walk in between | 2 x sets | 20 minutes |

Introduce some straight-line acceleration work and some curved runs if progressing well. Introduce these in separate sessions in case you react, and can therefore identify what activity caused the flare-up.

them as part of your dynamic warm-up to ensure that you are able to cope with the challenges of different movement patterns and to ensure a full physical recovery. See chapter 6 for some guidelines on different activities that would be suitable for this.

The key areas to remember with any acute injury are as follows:

- Follow the PRICE principle.
- Seek professional medical advice if the pain persists, or if you feel that the injury is severe (see a physician or a chartered physiotherapist).
- Maintain your fitness and conditioning via other modes of exercise that you are able to perform pain free (pool, bike, etc.).
- Time is a great healer; if it is too soon, rest and recover, and let your body do its work through the healing process.
- Begin a rehabilitation programme as soon as you feel safe to do so and are pain free.
- Don't just start off where you finished with your training, you will need to progressively load your body again to re-condition it and to reduce the incidence of chronic injuries.
- Listen to your body!

## Core function

Obviously as athletes we would much rather avoid injury altogether, rather than deal with the stress, pain and frustration of being injured. Many practitioners believe that core stability is an area that, if overlooked, can often cause problems in other areas of the body. Specifically, with poor core function, posture, and therefore gait and ultimately foot strike, can be impaired. Core stability or core function should be considered not only to aid performance, but also to minimise possible injury.

When we move, we place high torques and pressures on the human body and its systems.

What supports this load is the global functioning of the body as a whole, but, as the name suggests, the core of this is an essential component to balance, synergy and success.

The lumbo-pelvic hip region (*see* Figure 5.11) – also referred to as the core – is made up of a number of muscles:

- Rectus abdominis
- Transversus abdominis
- External oblique
- Internal oblique
- Multifidus
- Erector spinae
- Hip flexors
- Hip adductors
- Glutes
- Pelvic floor muscles

The effectiveness of these muscles working dynamically together will support the global movements of the body as a whole, especially when performing movements, like running.

The system of muscles is essentially an integrated sling system (*see* Figure 5.12), comprising several muscles, which produce force. The sling system is made up as shown, of anterior oblique, posterior oblique, lateral and longitudinal muscles.

A muscle may participate in more than one sling, and the slings may overlap and interconnect depending on the task being demanded. The hypothesis is that the slings have no beginning or end, but rather connect to assist in the transference of forces. It is possible that the slings are all part of one interconnected myofascial system and the particular sling (anterior oblique, posterior oblique, lateral, longitudinal) that is identified during any motion is merely due to the activation of selective parts of the whole sling.

Hodges and Richardson (1996) focused on the role of the transversus abdominis in healthy individuals, and the response of this muscle in patients with low back pain. Their research demonstrated that the transversus abdominis is an anticipatory muscle for stabilisation of the

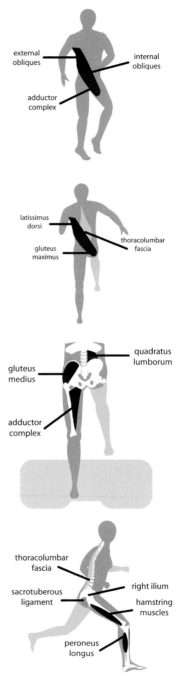

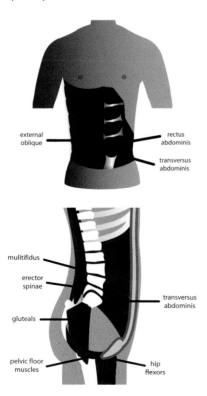

**Figure 5.11 Lumbo-pelvic hip region/core musculature**

**Figure 5.12 Sling system: anterior oblique, posterior oblique, lateral and longitudinal muscles.**

89

lower back, and is recruited prior to the initiation of any movement of the upper or lower extremity. The research also showed that this anticipatory recruitment of the transversus abdominis is absent or delayed in patients with low back pain. This leads to the hypothesis that, if you have low back pain, you possibly have a delayed firing of your transversus abdominis muscle – therefore, by training it, you should reduce low back pain.

Core-stability training begins with learning to co-contract the transverse abdominis (TA) muscle effectively, as this has been identified as key to the lumbar support mechanism, as stated by Hodges and Richardson (1996). By learning to activate your TA effectively you will ensure that your core is activated, which will protect the lumbar spine and pelvic region.

Because the muscles of the trunk and torso stabilise the spine from the pelvis to the neck and shoulder via the sling systems, they allow the transfer of powerful movements of the arms and legs. All powerful movements originate from the centre of the body out, and never from the limbs alone. Your core structure needs to be rigid and supportive to allow locomotion and movement. Indeed, the research from Hodge and Richardson indicates that by just moving your arm you activate your TA, unless your core function is compromised (TA delay).

In relation to running, Fredericson and Moore (2005) found that weakness or lack of sufficient

co-ordination in core musculature can lead to less efficient movements, compensatory movement patterns, strain and over-use, and injury. The research recommends that, for middle and long-distance runners whose events involve balanced and powerful movements of the body propelling itself forwards and catching itself in complex motor patterns, a strong foundation of muscular balance is essential.

This is where an effective core training programme comes in. This will help with creating a strong structure and musculature, and may also assist with any muscle imbalance, which may be identified in an assessment by a chartered physiotherapist or via the Functional Movement Screen (FMS)™.

Fredericson and Moore (2005) state that the purpose of basic core stabilisation exercises is not only to increase stability but, more importantly, to gain co-ordination and timing of the deep abdominal-wall musculature. It is extremely important to do these basic exercises correctly as they are the foundation of all other core exercises and movement patterns. These basic exercises emphasise maintaining the lumbar spine in a neutral position (which is the mid-range position between lumbar extension and flexion), allowing for the natural curvature of the spine.

This first stage of core stability training begins with the athlete learning to stabilise the abdominal wall. Proper activation of these muscles is considered crucial in the first stages of a core stability programme, before progressing to more dynamic and multi-planar activities. A number of basic exercises will teach you to activate and train your TA. It is important to be able to activate your TA effectively before progressing to more demanding movement patterns. There are a number of 'core' exercises that will help you achieve this – for instance, supine bent-knee raises, four-point kneeling (quadruped), four-point kneeling – alternate leg/arm raise, bridging, single-leg bridging, prone plank and side plank.

The core, lumbo-pelvic region and sling systems are complex structures within the body that are dynamic in nature. Much research and specialism is necessary for a full understanding of how the system works as a unit; for this reason, an in-depth analysis and discussion is beyond the scope of this book. Please refer to specialised core stability books and resources for more detailed information.

As Fredericson and Moore (2005) indicate, if an athlete has poor core control then they are more susceptible to injury, instability and low back pain. By committing to an effective core stability programme as part of your session you can ensure that your injury potential will be reduced and that you will be more efficient in your running economy.

## ACTIVATING YOUR TRANSVERSUS ABDOMINIS (TA)

The TA should always be activated prior to doing any core stability, or indeed any, exercise. One way to visualise 'turning on your TA' is as follows:

Imagine pulling in your belly button towards your spine with a piece of string while maintaining a neutral spine. Once you have pulled on the string, you should feel a slight tension and be able to continue to breathe normally.

Different triggers will work for different people. Another way to visualise this movement and activation is to imagine yourself stopping urinating mid-flow (don't actually do this, as it may cause a urine infection). This will activate the pelvic floor muscles, which will also trigger the TA as they work in unison.

No actual movement of the hip, spine or pelvis should occur with this movement; you should be able to hold the contraction without being rigid, and be able to talk and continue to breathe. It may take time to master, but is key to performing core stability and lifting exercises effectively.

# 6

# REST AND RECOVERY

When an athlete is training hard, rest is often as important as the training. Ron Hill may have been famous for always managing to run every day, but while this may have been part of the key to his marathon successes in 1970, we would not advocate this approach today.

## Recovery techniques

Recovery cannot be underestimated, and is essential in order to experience a safe and effective training and conditioning programme. Previously, when we have reviewed over-training and chronic injuries, they have had one thing in common: an inability to rest and recover will increase the incidence. If you don't recover well, your body will eventually break down.

Rest and recovery are all part of the package for optimal performance. This is the time when your body will become stronger from the stimulus you have thrown at it, but it needs to recover in order to do so. This is called 'supercompensation'. Supercompensation is when the body adapts to a training stimulus, recovers, adapts, then requires stimulation again. This is described by Vernon Gambetta (2007) as follows:

> *Supercompensation is a four-step process. The first step is the application of a training or loading stress and the body's subsequent reaction to this training stress, which is fatigue or tiring. There is a predictable drop-off in performance because of that stress. Step 2 is the recovery phase. This can be a lighter training session, a recovery session, or active rest. As a result of the recovery period, the energy stores and performance will return to the baseline (state of homeostasis) represented by the point of the application of the original training stress. Step 3 is the supercompensation phase. This is the adaptive rebound above the baseline; it is described as*

*a rebound response because the body is essentially rebounding from the low point of greatest fatigue. This supercompensation effect is not only a physiological response but also a psychological and technical response. The last step in the process is the loss of the supercompensation effect. This decline is a natural result of the application of a new training stress, which should occur at the peak of supercompensation. If no training stress is applied, there will also be a decline. This is the so-called detraining phenomenon.*

The process of training overload, supercompensation and recovery is discussed in a more detail in chapter 2, but the recovery element needs to be re-emphasised.

There are five main physiological components of fatigue as a result of intense exercise, which require an efficient recovery strategy. If these are neglected then the body may break down with an injury or illness, or you may underperform:

1 Nutrition
2 Hydration
3 Physical
4 Psychological
5 Neural

We will look at each of these in turn.

## Nutrition

As is discussed in Part 4 of this book, adequate and appropriate nutrition is the key to being able to train and compete successfully. Your glycogen (carbohydrate) stores will be depleted after exercise, so it is important to refuel effectively and get the timing right when you do so to ensure optimal nutrition and recovery. Both what and when to eat should become habit for the individual who wants to work hard and play hard. Do not underestimate the effect that good (or poor) nutrition has upon your ability to recover and perform on a daily basis.

## Hydration

Like nutrition, hydration is essential for success in your event (this, too, is covered in detail in Part 4). The body is made up of around 65 per cent water and a loss of just 2 per cent is claimed to reduce performance by 10–20 per cent, which is significant. A fluid loss exceeding 3–5 per cent of body weight impairs reaction time, judgement, concentration and decision making.

You may lose in excess of 2 kg of body fluid or sweat in a one-hour run or event (if not more in hot climates) and you need to make sure that you replenish this with approximately 1.25 litres of fluid per 1 kg of body weight lost. Therefore, if you lose 2 kg, you need to drink around 2.5 litres of fluid in addition to your normal fluid intake. Training yourself to consume that amount can be a challenge, with gastric bloating and frequent urination, but your body will adapt and it is important to maintain your levels of hydration at all times.

The volume of urine also indicates your level of hydration, your target being plenty of volume and straw-coloured urine. If you have low volume and dark, concentrated urine, then you are probably dehydrated. This is such a critical factor to performance and recovery that many elite athletes and professional teams monitor their level of hydration on a regular basis via a urinary osmometer – a device that indirectly assesses hydration levels by examining the concentration of your urine.

See the sections on (re)hydration in chapter 11 for more information on the various types of drinks available, and their pros and cons.

## Physical

The physical demands placed upon the body need to be considered and respected throughout training. When you exercise you actually damage the muscle fibres involved, the concept being that training will overload the body, you will go through the supercompensation phase, and then actually recover fitter and stronger. As a result, you can see that if you fail to allow your body to recover properly, your muscles just won't recover and you will feel chronically fatigued.

Muscle soreness, known as delayed onset muscle soreness (DOMS), usually occurs 12–48 hours post-exercise and is a normal physiological reaction to unaccustomed exercise, or if you haven't trained for a few weeks and start at your previous training level rather than gradually increasing your workload again.

DOMS may be perceived to be desirable by some people, as it indicates that the body has challenged itself and worked hard. Severe DOMS can be debilitating, however, causing the athlete to struggle to even walk properly. It can

also be milder, with that 'I feel that I worked hard yesterday' feeling, which is often desirable.

DOMS occurs more readily with eccentric exercise, where there are more micro-tears in the muscle fibres due to the nature of the activity. If you complete exercise that you are unaccustomed to, and don't recover fully, then you may increase the feeling of DOMS.

More research is needed on the subject, but ice baths, active recovery, contrast baths, stretching, compression garments and massage have all been attributed anecdotal benefits in relation to DOMS. The application of these is discussed in more detail later in this chapter. If the soreness doesn't go away after around four to five days then you may have injured yourself, in which case it would be advisable to seek professional medical advice.

## Psychological

Psychological fatigue may affect motivation and desire, as well as causing stress and frustration. Each individual is different in terms of their response to psychological fatigue, and their personality traits may affect how they react to certain situations and stimuli, depending on whether they are type A or type B personalities.

**Personality types**

- Type A: Hard-driving, ambitious, competitive
- Type B: Relaxed, easy-going

We saw from Wayne Keet's anecdote in chapter 4 that being a self-confessed type A personality drove him to over-training and severe immune system problems. Each athlete's perception of the same situation is different, with stress management techniques being highly individual. What is a serious physical challenge mentally to one athlete, is a breeze to another.

Relaxation techniques, visual imagery, breathing techniques, time management, yoga, massage, meditation and hypnosis may all help an athlete recover psychologically. Also, relaxing with friends over dinner or watching TV may be enough to help you wind down – everyone is different! What is important, though, is that you discover what you need in order to relax and give your mind a break. This works well with the concept of work–life balance and ensuring that you have areas of your life where you relax and recover. Your training is no different.

### Neural

With neural fatigue it is important to know that the central nervous system (CNS) experiences fatigue as a result of intense activity. When the athlete restores the CNS, which leads and co-ordinates all human activity, he or she will be able to concentrate better, perform skills correctly, react faster and more powerfully to internal and external stimuli, and subsequently maximise working capacity (Bompa, 1999).

The nervous system relies on glucose to function, just like the muscles, so if post-exercise and general nutrition is poor, then neural fatigue may occur, just like muscular fatigue (DOMS) may occur. The intensity of exer-cise can also lead to neural fatigue, with the motor neurons not firing as effectively as a result. This would potentially predispose the athlete to a higher risk of injury or an ineffective training programme, as muscle fibre recruitment may be affected.

Research in 1979 by Moritani and Devries indicated that, in relation to muscle strength gains after two weeks of training for a beginner, about 80 per cent of strength improvement could be attributed to increased muscle activation via neural factors, and only 20 per cent was due to changes in the muscle physiology itself. As training continued, the relative contribution of neural adaptation decreased, while the relative proportion of muscular contribution increased. This demonstrates the importance of the nervous system in muscular development and training.

## Rest days

Taking a rest day is no longer considered an option that is just for the weak. We would advocate at least one full rest day every week in order to allow muscular regeneration to occur. Ideally, this would mean getting as much rest as possible, not spending the day doing the gardening, walking round the shops for five hours or spring cleaning the house. To put it simply, why stand when you can sit? And, if you can, lie down rather than sit, and sleep if you get the chance. Take every opportunity you can to rest your legs. The same goes for the day pre-race.

In a similar vein, you need to consider ongoing rest. While we don't recommend a regimented periodisation to training, we do still advocate the need for rest within a training cycle. Ideally, runners should look to take one easy week in every four, and one easy, or rest, month every year.

## Tapering

Tapering is the term used when considering rest pre-competition. It is an essential component within a training and conditioning programme, and is crucial to achieving your best performance.

Conditioning and training damage the body, so reduced volume and intensity, as well as rest and recovery, are necessary in order to allow your body time to repair itself, to restore its energy sources and to prepare for competition. If you don't allow this to happen then you will under-perform and put yourself at risk of over-training and chronic injuries, as already discussed.

Interestingly, muscle strength increases significantly during the tapering period, and recent research indicates that a few days of rest or reduced training will not impair, and might even enhance, performance (Wilmore and Costill, 1994).

## Application of recovery principles

In addition to effective nutrition and hydration strategies that directly influence the body's ability to recover, there are other modes of recovery and applications that have been demonstrated over the years, either anecdotally or based upon research, to assist with the body's ability to recover effectively. These concepts have all been indicated to have a positive effect on an individual's ability to recover after intense exercise.

The Australian Institute of Sport recognises that there are a number of ways to enhance recovery from exercise, including:

- Rest and sleep
- Nutrition (*see* above and Part 4)
- Active recovery – warm-down and stretching (*see* also the section on flexibility in chapter 3)
- Massage
- Hydrotherapy – ice baths and contrast baths.

In addition to the above modes of recovery, we will also discuss the use of compression garments.

## Rest and sleep

Sounds simple doesn't it? Rest and sleep are simple yet effective ways for the body to recover after activity. Your room should be quiet, dark, cool and comfortable for optimal sleep, although there is an element of personal preference involved.

Walters (2002) discusses the five phases of sleep, with each stage leading to a more relaxed phase or physiological occurrence that helps the body repair and recover. Broadly defined, the stages of sleep occur as follows:

- **Stage 1:** Muscular relaxation.
- **Stage 2:** The body is closed off to the sound and sight of most external stimuli.
- **Stage 3:** Brainwaves vary, leading to stage 4.
- **Stage 4:** The deepest stage of sleep. This is as close to hibernation as humans ever

get. Stage 3 and 4 sleep, the deepest levels of sleep, are grouped together and are often referred to as slow-wave sleep.

- **Stage 5:** REM (rapid eye movement) occurs. During REM sleep, blood flow, pulse, respiration, body temperature and blood pressure all rise, and the eyes, underneath closed eyelids, dart back and forth as if scanning the environment. This is the stage in which dreams most commonly occur.

Although the body is continually in a process of revitalisation, this process peaks during stage 3 and 4 sleep (Martin, 1981). Two physiological events occur during slow-wave sleep that cause this effect. First, metabolic activity is at its lowest point and, second, the endocrine system increases the secretion of growth hormone via the pituitary gland. Growth hormone stimulates growth and repair in tissue, so is essential for effective recovery. If you don't sleep well or for long enough, and fail to reach stage 3 and 4 of your sleep phase then your body's ability to recover and regenerate may be compromised.

Everyone is different in terms of the volume of sleep they require, but ensure that you take what you need, and if your body tells you that it is tired, then it probably is!

## Active recovery: warm-down and stretching

The use of an active recovery or warm-down to accelerate recovery is well documented. It has been shown to be a much more effective way to recover than 'passive recovery', which is fundamentally sitting or standing, basically doing nothing to aid recovery after exercise.

It has been shown that an appropriate cool-down will:

- aid in the dissipation of waste products – including lactic acid;
- reduce the potential for DOMS;
- reduce the chances of dizziness or fainting caused by the pooling of venous blood at the extremities;
- reduce the level of adrenaline in the blood;
- allow the heart to return to its resting rate.

The warm-down should consist of 5–10 minutes of low-level aerobic-based activity or walking to lower the heart rate and help flush out the waste products resulting from exercise. It should be followed by some static stretches, which are appropriate during the cool-down as they help the muscles to relax, realign muscle fibres and re-establish their normal range of movement. These stretches should be held for approximately 5–10 seconds.

If you hold a stretch for too long, as you may want to in order to encourage muscle lengthening and developmental flexibility, rather than just realigning the muscle fibres after activity, you may well increase the micro-tears that have occurred during the session, and increase the incidence of muscle soreness.

## Massage

Massage is the systematic manipulation of soft body tissues; it assists in removing toxic energy metabolism by-products and residual fluid build-up resulting from the structural damage of muscle tissue (Bompa, 1999). Massage has been indicated to improve an athlete's mood by reducing tension, anger, fatigue, depression and anxiety. It will assist with increased blood and lymphatic circulation and drainage, which help to dissipate waste products, and encourages the circulation of fresh blood into the area. It may relieve muscle fatigue via the removal of metabolic by-products and excessive swelling (oedema), which is especially beneficial when treating certain types of inflammation (Cinque, 1989). Research indicates that massage has a positive effect on pain relief, muscle spasm and increased metabolism.

## Hydrotherapy: ice baths and contrast baths

Hydrotherapy is simply water therapy and has been used by people for hundreds of years. Whirlpools, water spas, Roman baths, your normal bath at home, and swimming pools are all examples of hydrotherapy. Water temperature, coupled with vibration or movement against the skin can be varied, and can soothe and relax muscles via hydrotherapy (in a Jacuzzi, for example).

It is proven that ice treatment (cryotherapy) decreases skin, subcutaneous and muscle temperature, causing narrowing of the blood vessels (vasoconstriction). This vasoconstriction has the beneficial effects of dulling and reducing the sensation of pain, limiting the amount of swelling, reducing muscle spasm and clearing metabolites from superficial to deep tissue. These are all desirable effects post-exercise.

Warmer water or heat induces vasodilation, drawing blood into the target tissues. Increased blood flow delivers oxygen and nutrients, and removes cell wastes. The warmth decreases muscle spasm, relaxes tense muscles, relieves pain and can increase the joints' range of motion.

Both techniques can be used via hydrotherapy. Two of the most common hydrotherapy modalities for athletes are discussed in more detail here.

### Ice baths

Having reviewed the PRICE principle, and noted the benefits of the application of ice to an acute injury (cold can provide short-term pain relief – it is an analgesic and also limits swelling by reducing blood flow), it is easy to see how having a post-exercise ice bath can be helpful for many athletes.

Again, much of the evidence is anecdotal, but some people swear by them! Research in the *British Journal of Sports Medicine* (Sellwood *et al.*, 2007) contradicts the idea that ice immersion is beneficial for an athlete's recovery post-exercise, but other studies and anecdotal evidence indicate that it is beneficial.

There may be a psychological benefit that accompanies the known analgesic effect of ice treatment, which of course is no doubt an individual preference. But if it gives you a sense of well-being post-immersion and you notice its positive effects during your next performance, then you are likely to praise its benefits.

The temperature of the bath should be between 10 and 15 degrees Celsius. There is no evidence to indicate that the colder the bath, the better it may be and, in fact, if the bath is too cold it can cause cold-induced muscle damage or fainting.

You should ensure that, once you are in the bath, you wiggle your legs around intermittently as a warm layer of water will collect around them, like a thermal layer, in order to keep you a bit warmer. If you move, it will feel colder.

The duration of immersion can be varied as there are a number of different protocols. For example:

- 1 x 10 minutes
- 2 x 5 minutes, 5 minutes out (good for teams when not many baths available)
- 2 minutes in, 2 minutes out x 5 (again, good for rotating groups of athletes)
- 1 minute in, 1 minute out x 8
- 4 minutes in, 2 minutes out x 3

About 12 kg of ice per person should be sufficient, although if you run the cold tap in your bath at home then it should be cold enough for you to benefit from the cold immersion. If you can add a few trays of ice from the freezer, then that should help too, but cold water alone may be of benefit. As noted above, the water will warm up as you sit in it, so you may have to run the cold tap every now and again to freshen it up.

Everyone is different and has a varying tolerance to the cold. Wear a towel around your shoulders or a jumper if necessary. Some athletes even wear neoprene boots to keep their toes and feet warm!

So, some people love ice baths and swear by them (Paula Radcliffe for one); others may put up with them, bearing the benefit to their training and performance in mind; others still may choose not to do them, and will not tolerate them at all. Everybody is different – but try one, you might like it!

If the end result is a feeling of freshness, recovery, regeneration and wellness – even psychologically, psychosomatically or due to a placebo effect – if it feels better for you, then it probably is better for you.

Something to be aware of with ice bath immersion is that there are contraindications. For example, if you have problems with cold – for example, a rheumatoid condition – then you should discuss the use of ice bath immersion with your physician prior to taking an ice bath.

**Contrast baths**

The theory is that contrast baths encourage a 'pumping' effect within the muscles, alternating vasoconstriction with vasodilatation.

For localised microtrauma associated with intense training, contrast baths have been shown to be effective for reducing stiffness and muscle soreness (Prentice, 1990). Prentice also suggests that contrast baths should begin and end with the cold treatment. The duration should be between 20 and 30 minutes, with the temperature of the cold being between 10 and 15 degrees Celsius and the hot being between 35 and 37 degrees Celsius.

# 3

# TRAINING DRILLS AND PROGRAMMES

# 7

# FUNCTIONAL DRILLS AND SESSIONS

So, now you know the basics. You know how to assess your training requirements via a needs analysis, you know how to prevent injury and, if you do get injured, you know how to treat it (PRICE), how to rehabilitate it and when to seek professional medical advice. You know how important it is to maintain your fitness, to look after your feet, and how and when to stretch.

The basics are there, and now you will want to complement your running programme with other functional drills, and strength and conditioning processes – running in itself will prepare you for running, but to enhance your performance, make you stronger and reduce the possibility of injury, it is advisable to complement your mileage runs with some strength and conditioning sessions.

## Running drills, speed and agility

Running drills, speed and agility will all assist in your running technique and running economy. These are also excellent for rehabilitation and can be used as part of your dynamic warm-up. They will increase hip and arm drive and co-ordination, which tend to exaggerate running mechanics so that, when you run, your muscle memory kicks in and you perform with good technique.

Speed, agility and running drills should be completed twice a week, ideally on grass or a running track. You should use them in your dynamic warm-up, and progress the intensity as you get warmer and more prepared for high-intensity activity. You can also introduce them during your rehabilitation from injury.

## DEFINITION: MUSCLE MEMORY

Muscle memory can best be described as a type of movement with which the muscles become familiar over time. Although the precise mechanism of muscle memory is unknown, what is theorised is that anyone learning a new activity, or practising an old one, has significant brain activity during this time. Muscle memory thus becomes an un-conscious process. The muscles grow accustomed to certain types of movement. This is extremely important in different types of training for sports. The more often you do a certain activity, the more likely you are to do it as and when needed.

The duration of the session doesn't need to be long. It is about quality, not quantity; 20- to 30-minute sessions are suitable, including the dynamic warm-up time. You can then continue with your normal training run after-wards.

There are a number of running and speed/agility drills that will enhance your running technique and performance. Figure 7.1 shows a number of examples to guide you. You should select maybe four or five different exercises to focus on for each session, and keep it varied. Perform each exercise three or four times over 30 m.

Figure 7.1 Running and speed/agility drills: high knees, skipping, high skips

Figure 7.1 (cont.)  Kick bum, carioca step, lunge steps, side slides, forward jockeys, backward jockeys, dynamic groins (in & out)

Figure 7.1 (cont.) Hamstring extensions, bounding, angled bounds, backward bounds, hopping (single leg)

## Strength training

Strength training is a great way to complement your running programme and improve your subsequent performance, in addition to having other positive effects on your body and wellness, as noted below. The benefits of strength training include:

- increased strength and power for sports performance;
- improved muscular development and body composition;
- injury prevention and rehabilitation;
- improved health;
- increased metabolism;
- improved flexibility and working range of movement;
- improved muscular endurance;
- improved balance and co-ordination;
- improved posture;
- improved sense of well-being and self-esteem.

You should complete your strength training with one or two rest days in between, to allow your body to recover and regenerate. So, you may complete your strength work on Monday, Wednesday and Friday, for example.

Even though running is an aerobic endurance event, you still require strength and power to enhance your performance and propel yourself along. Your legs will be strong because you run, but they are strong and efficient at carrying your body weight. If you load your body and improve your strength capacity then it makes sense that you will be able to propel yourself more efficiently and faster as a result of your increased strength gain.

In the past, athletes and coaches have been worried that increasing muscle mass will slow athletes down, and make them feel heavy and sluggish. As a result many athletes, and runners specifically, would choose not to lift weights. You only have to look at the Olympic track and field athletes to see that the lean, muscle-bound athletes are actually quite successful. The 100 m sprinters are extremely lean, with muscles pumping out of their bodies, as are the 1500 m runners, and 10 km and modern-day marathon runners. Having more muscle doesn't make you slow or cumbersome (as long as you do performance lifting rather than body-building). It makes you more powerful, more explosive and more resistant to injury.

It is a common misconception that lifting weights and gaining strength may slow you down. Research by Wisløff *et al.* (2004) indicates that there is a high correlation between squat strength, vertical jump and sprint performance. Although this research was carried out specifically with football players, it is obvious that an improvement in strength that leads to an improvement in sprint performance would be beneficial in most sports, including running.

It is desirable for elite runners to maintain a low body mass, but this shouldn't compromise their ability to improve body strength. Indeed, most elite middle- or long-distance runners' morphology and genetic potential would not predispose them to the type of hypertrophy that a 100 m runner may experience. The middle- and long-distance runner may focus on muscular endurance initially, then progress to predominately strength-based sessions, which is important for achieving an improvement in running economy, as discussed below.

If you are a member of your local gym, you may already complete some resistance or strength training. Most gyms have a plethora of resistance equipment, weight machines and free weights areas.

When the gym and health club boom occurred in the 1980s, resistance machines offered an easy and safe way for the masses to complete resistance and strength training. People would sit on a machine and perform the exercise, the benefit being that the risk of injury or incorrect movement patterns was limited, so resistance training was accessible to all.

This is still the case in many health clubs and gyms, and although sitting on a machine completing a certain amount of sets and repetitions is acceptable for some people, as far as performance strength training is concerned, it isn't as functional and doesn't challenge the body as globally as using free weights does.

When you run, your entire body is working as a unit. There is not one isolated muscle group doing the work – you are a global unit propelling yourself along. It therefore makes sense that the strength exercises of choice should challenge your body in the same way, by being dynamic, global, multi-joint movements in order to condition your body for the transfer from strength training in the gym or at home to your running performance. An example of a global movement pattern that transfers well to runners would be a high pull or clean. Purely by the nature of the movement pattern and the muscle recruitment, you can see how these exercises will improve strength, movement, co-ordination and running economy (*see* page 112 and the photo sequence below).

However, some free weights exercises and lifts are very technical and challenging, and good technique is an essential component of success. It is important to ensure that ineffective or unsafe movement patterns are not completed as this would potentially lead to poor posture and increased injury potential. These more complex movement patterns should be monitored by a strength and conditioning coach or an exercise professional.

There are, however, many free weight movements that you can do that are extremely safe and will challenge your co-ordination and body movement; this will enhance your body awareness and, subsequently, your running speed.

Another positive aspect of free weights is that, to begin with, you don't need any equipment. You can complete the exercises purely with your own body weight. As you get stronger you will need to overload your system, as you would with your running intensity, but initially you can create your own programme at home, so there are no excuses!

Indeed, your imagination may be the limiting factor with strength training, as there are many training means to provide external resistance and improve performance. For example:

- Body weight
- Medicine balls
- Elastic bands and cords
- Dumbbells
- Barbells.

When you complete strength training it is important to select the correct prescription, this being sets and repetitions. This is based on your training goals as well as training experience. As we discussed earlier, the initial gain in strength is via neural development and co-ordination, with actual muscular recruitment occurring a few weeks into your programme.

Strength training prescription is based upon the following principles:

- The higher the load (weight or resistance), the lower the number of repetitions.
- The lower the load (weight or resistance), the higher the number of repetitions.

Often, the load is recorded as a percentage of maximum strength. With elite athletes, where the strength and conditioning coach may work out the 1RM or 3RM (repetition maximum, *see* below), this offers an accurate way of over-loading and challenging them.

If you are new to strength training, then another effective way is to work to your 'repetition maximum' (RM). For example, you may choose to lift 12 repetitions to achieve an improvement in muscular endurance and hypertrophy, so – to work at your RM – you would need to 'feel the burn' on the final three or four repetitions, and just about be able to squeeze out the final repetition in order to benefit from overload, but always maintaining good form and technique. You will find that, after a few sessions, you will need to increase the load to benefit from the same effect. In simple terms, this is effective strength training!

## DEFINITIONS: REPS AND SETS

- Repetitions ('reps'): the number of lifts or movements within a set.
- Sets: a set consists of the prescribed number of repetitions for an exercise, followed by a period of rest.

If you can perform the lift or movement without any muscular fatigue at the end of the set, then you need to increase the load or manipulate the sets and reps.

The number of sets and repetitions can be manip-ulated so that you can achieve your specific training goals. For an individual who is new to lifting weights then it is a generally accepted protocol for them to begin with performing three sets of 12-15 repetitions in order to gain some muscular endurance adaptation, hypertrophy and general muscular conditioning. As the individual adapts and 'overloads' the muscles appropriately they will soon need to increase the load lifted to continue with the benefits of training.

Once the technique of lifting has been mastered and the body has adapted, then the protocol that is used will need to be changed. Table 7.1 provides a guideline as to how many sets and repetitions one should use in order to achieve specific training goals.

You should use table 7.1 as a guideline to help you to decide what sets and reps and rest you require for your strength programme, and then determine the subsequent/adequate load needed to experience the RM. If you have access to a strength and conditioning coach or exercise profes-sional then they will prescribe accordingly and may use %1RM or %3RM as an alternate to RM.

## Strength training: research for runners

Research by Johnston *et al.* (1995) discusses strength training in relation to running economy.

**Table 7.1 Resistance training guidelines**

| Training goal | Number of sets | Number of repetitions | Rest between sets |
|---|---|---|---|
| Muscular endurance | 3-4 | 12-15 RM | 30-60 seconds |
| Muscular hypertrophy | 3-5 | 8-12 RM | 60-90 seconds |
| Strength | 3-5 | Heavy resistance ⩽ 6 RM | 2 minutes |
| Power | 3-5 | 1-5 RM | 2 minutes |

## DEFINITIONS: STRENGTH, ENDURANCE AND HYPERTROPHY

- Strength: the quality or state of being strong – capacity for exertion or endurance.
- Endurance: the ability to sustain a prolonged stressful effort or activity.
- Hypertrophy: the excessive development of an organ or part; specifically increase in bulk (as by thickening of the muscle fibres) without multiplication of part.

The research introduced a 10-week strength training programme to some distance runners who had no previous experience with strength training.

Over the 10-week period they performed strength training exercises three times a week for the 10-week trial. The programme was progressed as necessary to ensure that the runners performed to their RM; it used strength-based repetitions, and did not focus on endurance or hypertrophy. Repetitions started at between 10RM and 12RM in weeks one to three and progressed to 6RM to 8RM in weeks four to eight, finishing in the last two weeks of the 10-week block at between 4RM and 6RM. The results of the study found that the runners improved their running economy by 4 per cent within the 10-week programme.

Running economy is defined as the steady-state oxygen consumption (ml/kg/min) for a standardised running speed. By improving their running economy, a runner should be able to run faster over the same distance or run longer at the same running speed, due to decreased oxygen consumption. The study noted no effect on aerobic capacity or blood lactate accumulation, and the participants in the study continued to follow their normal running routine.

## Exercise selection

There are many exercises that will improve your strength gain and, as a result, improve your running economy and performance. Figure 7.2 shows some examples to guide you in your selection. They are general, all-over body (global, multi-joint) exercises that will improve your overall level of conditioning and strength, as well as assist with injury prevention.

All these exercises can be performed with body weight to begin with, and progressed to use dumbbells or barbells as you get stronger.

**Figure 7.2 Strength training exercises: squat, split squat, lunge, good morning exercise**

Figure 7.2 (cont.) Deadlift, calf raise, squat calf raise, single leg squat, high pull

Figure 7.3 Plyometrics-based exercises: Bounding, Hopping, Pike jump, Standing jumps, Tuck jumps

Figure 7.3 (cont.) Box jump (off); Box jump (on); Cone jumps (forwards & sideways)

results of the research clearly demonstrated that a six-week plyometric programme led to improvements in 3 km running performance; the rationale was based on an improvement in running economy, much like the strength-based research by Johnston *et al.* (1995).

The number of sets and repetitions of plyometrics should be carefully monitored and graduated to ensure there is no increased risk of injury.

The number of foot 'contacts' is normally measured during plyometric training to ensure that the load is not too intense or high, and is appropriately graduated. Initially, for a beginner, foot contacts should be around 60–100, progressing to between 100 and 150 contacts for more intermediate athletes and those who are more accustomed to the drills.

Drills should be varied and, as always, should be performed with quality rather than quantity. Intensity is the key: the more dynamic the exercise and the greater the power generated, the fewer foot contacts are required. Rest between sets should be between one and two minutes.

## Resisted and hill running

Resisted and hill running can improve acceleration, develop the muscular system and increase stride length. The 'overspeed' that occurs to your muscles when you release the resistance cord, or sprint down a hill, will cause your muscles to fire at a quicker rate and recruit more muscle fibres. Common

methods of resisted training include running in water, running with parachutes, running uphill, running up steps, pulling weighted sleds and running while harnessed with stretch cords.

Stride frequency is best improved through overspeed training methods, such as being towed with stretch cords, running downhill (1- to 5-degree slopes), running in sand and running on treadmills at high speeds.

In hill running, the athlete is using their body weight as a resistance to push against, so the driving muscles from which their leg power is derived have to work harder. Hill work results in the calf muscles learning to contract more quickly, and thereby generating work at a higher rate as they become more powerful. The calf muscle achieves this by recruiting more muscle fibres, around two or three times as many when compared to running on the flat. Hill training offers the following benefits. It:

- helps develop power and muscle elasticity;
- improves stride frequency and length;
- develops co-ordination, encouraging the proper use of arm action during the driving phase and feet in the support phase;
- develops control and stabilisation, as well as improved speed (downhill running);
- promotes strength endurance;
- develops maximum speed and strength (short hills);
- improves lactate tolerance (mixed hills).

You need a hill or some steps, which are easy enough to find, but for some of the exercises you will need a bungee cord, sled or parachute in addition to a partner to hold them, which may be a limiting factor.

Excellent running technique must be maintained at all times. Do not perform the exercise if it compromises your running technique. Again, as these sessions are complex, it is advisable to consult a strength and conditioning specialist or exercise professional prior to commencing them.

The following sections give some examples of resisted drills and hills runs.

### Resisted sprints
Distance: 5–20 m
Repetitions: 4–8
Rest: 2 minutes between each repetition

Partner assisted with a bungee cord or resistance trainer (non-elastic). Attach the bungee or resistance trainer as indicated by the specific equipment instructions; always ensure safety as injury can occur if the device is not used correctly. Once secure, the individual who is working (the 'worker') will begin their run over the selected distance, with the partner holding the bungee or resistance trainer to create sufficient torque, so the worker has to overcome some resistance and 'power' through the sprint. The worker should power the arms, lean slightly forwards, looking upright, and produce a good knee lift, maintaining excellent running technique throughout the selected distance.

The partner will follow the worker over the selected distance, and maintain an effective resistance with the bungee or resistance trainer throughout the selected distance.

### Contrast sprints: resisted/non-resisted
Resisted distance: 5–20 m
Non-resisted distance: 10–30 m
Repetitions: 4–8
Rest: 2 minutes between each repetition

Partner resisted with a bungee cord or resistance trainer (non-elastic). Instructions as above for the resisted sprints, and ensure safety at all times. Once the resisted distance has been covered by the worker, the partner, or worker (depending on the specific device), releases the bungee cord or resistance trainer, and the runner/worker covers the non-resisted distance as fast as possible, maintaining excellent technique, powering the arms, with excellent leg drive, leaning slightly forwards.

### Hill running
Find a short hill with an incline of between 5 and 15 degrees' gradient. As with the work in the resisted running sessions, you should ensure that you perform the hill runs with excellent technique: leaning slightly forwards, powering the arms, good knee drive, looking forwards throughout the selected distance. Perform the following according to your requirements:

- 8–10 repetitions over 50 m
- 8–10 repetitions over 150 m
- 8–10 repetitions over 200 m

You should walk back for your recovery, and ensure that your work-to-rest ratio is at least three to five times the duration of the run.

All the above sessions should be maximal, and always performed when fresh and with excellent technique. Ensure that you have enough rest in between each repetition, and perform them at the beginning of a session, when you are least fatigued.

# 8

# TRAINING PROGRAMME DESIGN

## Putting it all into practice: exercise prescription

Planning your training week can be the final challenge. Although you will have reviewed your needs analysis and ensured that you are committed in order to reach your training targets, the reality of how it all fits into your week can be quite daunting.

Your training programme is something that you plan many months in advance of a major race. It is virtually impossible to set out a programme lasting six or eight months and to be able to perform every session as planned. Indeed, it would be misguided to force yourself to follow such a programme as it would mean ignoring signs of over-training, and would probably lead to illness or injury. The point of building a training programme is to create a guide aimed

at bringing you to peak condition for your chosen event.

The training programme is not a template to be followed blindly, but more the framework of a jigsaw into which you will fit the pieces over the coming months. After each week of your programme you should allocate time to assess how you have performed, and be ready to alter your next week's schedule accordingly. Below are two scenarios to help you visualise how your week may look based upon your training goals and commitments.

Example 1 (table 8.1) is based on running or training three times a week. It includes 2 x speed/agility/running drill sessions, 3 x strength sessions and 3 x runs. You can slot in an additional run within a rest day quite easily,

**Table 8.1 Training programme: example 1**

| Monday | Tuesday | Wednesday | Thursday | Friday | Saturday | Sunday |
|---|---|---|---|---|---|---|
| REST DAY | Speed/agility running drills | REST DAY | | Speed/agility running drills | REST DAY | |
| | **Run** | | **Run** | | | **Run** |
| | Strength session | | Strength session | | | Strength session |

Recovery after each training session

but remember to have your rest days. The days that you train are very easy to change around depending on work and family commitments, which provides great flexibility.

Example 2 (table 8.2) is a more demanding schedule. It still has 2 x speed/agility/running drills and 3 x strength sessions, but includes 5 x running days and 2 x rest days.

As you can see, most of the rest days are slotted in after two or three consecutive days' activity, to allow the body to adapt and recover efficiently.

Pool or bike sessions can be added in as necessary for either conditioning/training or recovery, again depending upon your schedule and training goals. The intensity and duration of the running sessions can be manipulated according to how you are periodising and planning your

training, where you are in your training cycle and when your event is.

Many people find visual cues really helpful, especially if training and running are relatively new to them. If this is the case for you, write out a schedule, similar to the ones above, and pop it on the fridge or pin it up at work to encourage your adherence and help you achieve your goals. Having a training partner will also help to ensure that you get things done.

Remember: recovery is part of your training and should be considered when planning your training week and time allocation.

## Building your training programme

We have set out two more detailed training plan structures for you to use and adapt to your own circumstances. The programmes are for an

**Table 8.2 Training programme: example 2**

| Monday | Tuesday | Wednesday | Thursday | Friday | Saturday | Sunday |
|---|---|---|---|---|---|---|
| REST DAY | Speed/agility running drills | | Speed/agility running drills | REST DAY | | |
| | **Run** | Run | **Run** | | **Run** | **Run** |
| | Strength session | | Strength session | | Strength session | |

Recovery after each training session

advancing runner and an accomplished runner. The actual sessions are not vitally important – it is the methodology behind the creation of the programme that carries more value.

All the training that we propose is based on time spent training rather than distance covered, and requires you to use the training zones, or training sensations, described in chapter 2. In this way, as your fitness increases, the intensity you work at will remain appropriate to your physiology, and your pace should gradually improve.

## The advancing athlete

The advancing runner is one that has some running experience but has not yet tackled a longer-distance running event. For the advancing runner attempting their first big event we shall assume that their aim is to finish, or finish towards the middle of the event.

You should aim to build up the time spent training in three-week cycles.

Start off with a level of training you are comfortable with, then aim to add time to sessions the next week. The third week in the cycle should be a recovery week in which you reduce the volume of training to less than the first week in the cycle. In this way you give your body time to regenerate and adapt to the increased stress being placed upon it.

This phase builds key elements of fitness. The main focus is development of the endurance base, but the Sunday effort starts to get the athlete used to running towards race-pace efforts.

Additionally, these sessions should include a warm-up and warm-down period of between 10 and 20 minutes, and ideally, at least twice per

**Table 8.3 Base endurance/build phase (advancing athlete)**

| Phase duration | 1–3 months, ideally |
|---|---|
| Training time | 3–6 hours per week |
| Aim | This phase is about getting you to spend more time running and getting used to training regularly |
| Monday | REST |
| Tuesday | END zone 30–60 minutes |
| Wednesday | REST or R&B zone 15–20 minutes as easy recovery run |
| Thursday | END zone 30–75 minutes |
| Friday | REST |
| Saturday | END zone 40–90 minutes |
| Sunday | Easy club run of 60–120 minutes – don't worry about your training intensity, enjoy the time running with others if possible |

week, should include speed and agility running following the warm-up. Strength sessions can be added following endurance running days on Wednesday and Sunday.

The final week before race day should reduce this workload even further, with nothing but easy recovery runs in the final three days before the race.

## The accomplished runner

The accomplished runner is one that has a solid racing background and several years of training and competition. Their aim will be to improve on

**Table 8.4 Base endurance phase (advancing athlete)**

| | |
|---|---|
| Phase duration | 12– to 16–week training block |
| Training time | 4–8 hours per week |
| Aim | To build up volume of endurance training and fitness |
| Monday | REST |
| Tuesday | END zone 45–75 minutes |
| Wednesday | R&B zone 20–40 minutes |
| Thursday | END zone 45–90 minutes |
| Friday | REST |
| Saturday | END zone 60–120 minutes |
| Sunday | Long group run of gradually increasing effort from 60 minutes to 2 hours |

previous performances and they will be prepared to commit more time to training than those in the improving athlete category. We shall assume that the focus of this athlete's forth-coming season is a marathon-distance event.

As the accomplished runner is likely to be undertaking a reasonably high volume of training, it may be necessary to carry out two training sessions on some days. But always remember that it is not an aim to clock up as many hours as you can – always be conscious of how you are recovering between sessions, and adjust your training accordingly.

This phase could be based on a four-week cycle with three weeks of adding volume followed by a recovery week. If you feel capable of coping

**Table 8.5 Transition phase (advancing athlete)**

| | |
|---|---|
| Phase duration | 6– to 8–week threshold training block to start 10 weeks before race day |
| Training time | Variable |
| Aim | To build on endurance base and introduce threshold sessions*; volume decreases but intensity increases; threshold sessions aimed at improving race pace |
| Monday | REST |
| Tuesday | ThT zone – sessions as below |
| Wednesday | END zone 60–120 minutes |
| Thursday | ThT zone – sessions as below |
| Friday | REST |
| Saturday | ThT zone – sessions as below |
| Sunday | END or R&B session of 2–3 hours (shorter if race focus is 5 km to 21 km) |

* Threshold sessions can be:

- 2 or 3 efforts of 12 minutes, with 8 minutes recovery; or
- 3–5 efforts of 8 minutes, with 6 minutes recovery; or
- 4–8 efforts of 5 minutes with 3 minutes recovery.

## Table 8.6 Taper phase (advancing athletes)

| | |
|---|---|
| Phase duration | 3 weeks pre-event (repeated twice) |
| Training time | Variable |
| Aim | To allow full recovery prior to race day and use short, high-intensity sessions to build some more speed |
| Monday | REST |
| Tuesday | S&P hill efforts – 4–6 maximal efforts of 20–30 seconds with 5 minutes walk/jog recovery |
| Wednesday | Rest or R&B run of 30 minutes |
| Thursday | ThT/S&P session of 6 (then 4) x 1 km efforts at target race pace with 3 minutes recovery |
| Friday | REST |
| Saturday | ThT session of 2 or 3 efforts of 8 minutes with 2 minutes recovery |
| Sunday | END run of 90–120 minutes |

with more you can introduce a 'crash week' on the third week of the build phase, where you put in a really tough week before the rest week. This accentuates the training response caused by the excessive overload, but there are risks involved. Crash weeks put a lot of strain on the body and may leave you susceptible to colds or viruses, as they may temporarily weaken your immune system. This means that extra attention must be paid to nutrition and recovery between sessions during these crash weeks.

**Table 8.7 Base volume training (accomplished runner)**

| | |
|---|---|
| Phase duration | Ideally a minimum of 3 months |
| Training time | 8–16 hours per week |
| Aim | To build cardiovascular base fitness, and improve endurance capacity and running economy |
| Monday | REST |
| Tuesday | AM – 30–60-minute R&B zone run<br>PM – 60–90-minute END zone |
| Wednesday | AM – 30–90-minute R&B zone<br>PM – Rest or R&B zone 20–40 minutes and strength work |
| Thursday | AM – 30–60-minute R&B run<br>PM – 90 minute to 2 hours END zone and strength work |
| Friday | 30–45-minute R&B recovery session |
| Saturday | 90 minutes to 2 hours END zone and possible strength session |
| Sunday | 60 minutes to 2 hours club run, mixed pace or increasing pace effort |

These sessions should be performed with a warm-up and warm-down of a minimum of 15 minutes, but possibly as long as 30 minutes, and should also incorporate the speed and agility drills following warm-up.

The accomplished athlete who is looking to increase their training load may add a second session on a daily basis so long as sufficient recovery is being gained. This could be either 20–40 minutes of R&B, or 30–60 minutes of END, depending on the athlete's needs.

**Table 8.8 Threshold training block (accomplished runner)**

| | |
|---|---|
| Phase duration | 8–12 weeks, continue until 3 weeks before race day |
| Training time | Variable |
| Aim | To introduce threshold training sessions* – improve race pace |
| Monday | REST or ThT – 6–8 efforts of 5 minutes with 1 minute recovery |
| Tuesday | R&B – 45–120 minutes with strength work |
| Wednesday | END – 90–150 minutes |
| Thursday | S&P – hill sprints or sustained efforts of 3 minutes, all with 3–5 minutes full recovery |
| Friday | REST |
| Saturday | AM – END – 90–120 minutes<br>PM – ThT session, as below |
| Sunday | Long group run of mixed or increasing pace |

* Alternative threshold sessions can be any one of the following:

- 2–4 efforts of 12 minutes with 3 minutes recovery
- 3–5 efforts of 8 minutes with 2 minutes recovery
- 4–8 efforts of 5 minutes with 1 minute recovery.

The final week before race day should reduce this workload even further, with nothing but easy recovery sessions in the final three days before the race.

**Table 8.9 Taper phase (accomplished runner)**

| Phase duration | 3-week taper phase |
|---|---|
| Training time | Variable |
| Aim | To allow the athlete to recover, and ensure peak fitness on race day |
| Monday | REST |
| Tuesday | S&P session 12 x 400 m efforts with 1–2 minutes recovery |
| Wednesday | END run of 45–60 minutes |
| Thursday | S&P session 4 x 30-second hill efforts with 3 minutes walk recovery |
| Friday | 45–60-minute easy R&B run |
| Saturday | ThT effort – 6 x 5 minutes, 1 minute rest |
| Sunday | END 90–120 minutes |

## Adapting the training programmes for other distances

These plans are not to be followed rigidly – they give an idea of the training structure that we would propose. Essentially this book is about giving you the knowledge to be able to coach yourself, so it should be quite easy for you to take the training principles we have set out and adapt them to other distances. Although the structure of your training programme will change, the basic principles remain the same. The importance of recovery, of training within your specified training zones and of paying attention to nutrition is all the same. The shorter the event you are focusing on, the greater the need for higher-intensity sessions in addition to endurance. The longer you are racing, the more the importance of speed diminishes and the importance of running economy (and therefore total running time) increases.

# 4

# NUTRITION

# 9

# GENERAL NUTRITION

While adequate and appropriate training may be the key to optimal race-day performance, adequate and appropriate nutrition is the key to being able to train successfully.

Consider again the analogy of the Formula One car and the distance runner (*see* Figure 2.1). To be able to complete the race distance, the car needs sufficient fuel. To be competitive in the race, the car needs to use the highest-quality fuel in an optimal way. This needs to be of a type to provide enough power for the duration of the race and to be used efficiently. If the car is powered by diesel instead of high-octane race fuel the level of performance will be reduced.

As with the high-performance car, the fuel required to power the endurance runner must be of the right type if that individual is to achieve their optimum performance. However, unlike a Formula One car, the human body has not one, but three sources of energy: carbohydrate, fat and protein. It is important that, in order to achieve optimal performance for sport, these fuel sources are consumed in the correct quantity and at the most appropriate time.

## Basic dietary needs

Before considering what is important for the exercising individual, it is important to fully understand the basic nutritional requirements of the body. Good nutrition is essential to good health and the prevention of disease. At rest, the requirement is to supply the body with sufficient nutrients for energy, for building and maintaining body tissue (growth and repair), and for the maintenance of metabolic processes. In order to do this, we must supply our body with an adequate supply of macronutrients (carbohydrate, fat and protein), micronutrients (vitamins and minerals) and water.

## Carbohydrate

Carbohydrate is the body's primary energy source as it is broken down more completely and efficiently than fat or protein. This role is twofold: to provide energy for activity, and to provide a constant supply of blood glucose for functioning of the brain and the central nervous system. Because of this, the absolute minimum requirement of carbohydrate intake is 100 g per day, although the recommended minimum intake of carbohydrate for the non-exercising adult is 130 g per day.

The secondary role of carbohydrate is to spare protein. When the carbohydrate supply is inadequate, protein is broken down to glucose. In this case, the key function of protein is suppressed and protein is converted to ensure blood glucose is maintained.

The final function of carbohydrate is in the metabolism of fat. Fat burning occurs more completely and efficiently when sufficient carbohydrates are available. Without an adequate supply of carbohydrate, fat breakdown is incomplete, and the resultant ketones will lead to fatigue, nausea, lack of appetite and, in extreme cases, coma or even death.

The recommended target for carbohydrate intake is 55–60 per cent of calorific requirements for the normal individual. Additionally, to ensure health, no more than 25 per cent of daily calorie intake should come from sugars.

## Fat

While considered by many as an unwelcome addition to the diet, fat has many key roles and therefore must not be overlooked.

The primary function of fat is as a source of energy, secondary to the energy released from carbohydrate. Despite containing twice the energy of carbohydrates, fat isn't the preferred fuel of the body as it is slower and more difficult to metabolise. However, while the body cannot store large amounts of carbohydrate, stored fat in adipose cells provides the largest and most efficient store of energy in the body, and therefore can provide almost limitless energy.

Additionally, fat has several other key roles, which include, most importantly, the provision of a source of several key fat-soluble vitamins and essential fatty acids, which cannot be manufactured by the body. Fat also helps to protect vital organs, acts as a source of insulation and is a lubricant for body tissue.

From a dietary perspective, fat adds moisture to food, making it more palatable and pleasant to consume. For this reason, it is often easy to overindulge in high-fat foods. Ideally the fat intake in your diet should provide between 20 and 35 per cent of the calories consumed, with less than 10 per cent of your total calories coming from saturated fats.

## Protein

While carbohydrate and fat are the predominant energy sources in the body, the role of protein

## TIPS TO REDUCE DIETARY FAT INTAKE

- Reduce the use of butter/margarines on sandwiches or toast (occasionally go without – it won't take long before you don't notice the difference).
- Consume lower-fat milk. (While the difference between 2 per cent and 4 per cent is small, this actually accounts for 20 g of fat in 1 litre of milk!)
- Use low-fat or fat-free salad dressing.
- Adopt low-fat cooking methods – avoid frying if possible, and grill, bake or steam your food instead.
- Choose tomato-based sauces or low-fat sauces rather than butter or cream-based sauces for pasta, rice or potatoes.
- Learn to read food labels. Processed and pre-packaged 'ready meals' can often have very high fat content.

is slightly different. Although protein does have an energy yield, and can be used to provide energy to sustain metabolism should carbohydrate stores become depleted, protein is mainly required for normal growth and development of the body structures and tissue.

Proteins form a part of every living cell, and differ from fat and carbohydrate in that they also contain nitrogen, in addition to carbon, oxygen and hydrogen. Protein itself is made of smaller organic compounds called amino acids. It has been suggested that the body contains over 50,000 different proteins, although only about 1000 have been identified. Each specific protein is determined by the number, arrangement and variety of amino acids that it contains. Hence amino acids are often known as 'building blocks'.

Classification of amino acids is referred to as either essential or non-essential. The non-essential amino acids can be synthesised in the liver in sufficient quantities to maintain health, however essential amino acids can't be manufactured by the body and must be acquired from dietary intake. All essential amino acids must be available in sufficient quantities at all times to ensure adequate synthesis of vital proteins. Insufficient quantities of essential amino acids will lead to health-related problems.

Dietary proteins are further classified as complete proteins (for example, meat, milk, cheese and eggs) when they contain enough of all the essential amino acids in sufficient quantity to maintain tissue and support growth. Incomplete proteins lack one or more of the essential amino acids that the body needs. This does not mean that such food should be avoided, as a mixture of incomplete proteins will combine to meet the bodily requirements. Generally speaking, complete proteins are from animal sources, and incomplete proteins come from plant-based foods. Eating a variety of foods is recommended in order to ensure all the amino acids are obtained.

The specific function of the individual protein is dependent on its composition of various amino acids. However, there are several major functions of proteins in the body. Primarily, proteins are vital for the maintenance, growth and repair of body tissue. They are also vital in the regulation of body processes, being essential in the manufacture of hormones and enzymes. They function within the immune system, creating specific antibodies to give protection from infection and disease, as well as assisting in blood clotting. Plasma proteins function in the regulation of body fluid and electrolyte balance. Finally, if carbohydrate or fat levels are inadequate, proteins can be used as an energy source.

To meet the basic needs of health, the recommended daily allowance of protein is 0.8 g for each kilogram of the individual's body weight, and should provide a minimum of 10 per cent of daily energy intake. While this may be appropriate for the non-exercising individual, the needs of the endurance runner will be reviewed later.

## Micronutrients

The term micronutrient, which is commonly used to describe vitamins and minerals, is used to refer to the fact that these nutrients are needed in very small quantities. Although neither is a source of energy, vitamins and minerals are also a crucial part of the diet.

## Vitamins

The key role of vitamins is to facilitate the chemical reactions in the body associated with normal metabolism, growth and development. Each vitamin has a very specific function that cannot be substituted by other compounds. Therefore, as vitamins cannot be manufactured by the body and vitamin function is specific, appropriate intake is crucial to well-being. When vitamin intake is inadequate this will not only impact on normal bodily function, but can also result in longer-term health issues.

Vitamins are classified as either water soluble or fat soluble. The group of vitamins termed 'water soluble', since they are found in the watery portion of food, are absorbed directly into the bloodstream. Since they are held in solution, they are not stored and therefore need to be consumed daily. Vitamin C and the B complex vitamins are water soluble. When consumed in excess, this classification of vitamins is excreted in urine, although excess intake can be toxic.

Vitamins classified as fat soluble are, as the name suggests, absorbed with fats, and can be stored in the liver or the adipose (fat) tissue within the body. Because of the ability of the body to store these vitamins, daily intake is not required. Fat-soluble vitamins are A, D, E and K. Excess intake of these vitamins, particularly A and D, can have serious consequences, including liver or kidney damage.

The guidelines set by nutrition experts for recommended daily intakes (RDIs) of vitamins are sufficient for both the 'normal' and athletic population. Furthermore, despite heavy marketing from supplementation companies, vitamins are found in all major food groups, and therefore intake from a healthy and varied diet should be sufficient to meet the individual's needs. Where an individual does not have an additional, medically defined, need for vitamins, and yet still desires to use supplements, these should be consumed only at a level no more than the RDA (recommended daily allowance).

### Minerals

Minerals are inorganic substances that are required for promoting growth and maintaining health. Unlike vitamins, they become part of the body structure, making up approximately 4 per cent of total body weight, and are found in all tissues and body fluids.

Minerals are essential to diet as they have two key functions. Their first role is providing structural support, by giving strength to bones, teeth, skin, hair and nails. Their second role is a regulatory function, as specific minerals are involved with maintaining fluid balance, nerve cell transmission and muscle contraction.

Minerals are found in all major food groups, however both excessive and insufficient mineral intake can cause health problems. Calcium and sodium intakes currently appear to cause the biggest problem in the western world. As with all the other nutrients, a healthy and varied diet will provide the appropriate intake and supplementary sources should not be required.

## Water balance

The final consideration in our discussion about general dietary requirements is water. As water constitutes around 60–65 per cent of the total body weight of the adult male, and approximately 50–55 per cent of the body weight of the adult female, ensuring adequate hydration is one of the most basic nutritional requirements. Yet it is often overlooked.

Water is lost in several ways. Fluid is lost through sweat – during both warm weather and exercise – and also through excretion. Insensible water loss also occurs, mostly through the breath but also through the skin. It is easy to become moderately dehydrated over a number of days. Without water intake a person can survive for no longer than a week – without food they can survive a month!

Water is essential as it has many functions. It:

- gives shape to cells;
- helps form the structure of large molecules, such as glycogen and protein;
- serves as a lubricant in mucus secretions and joint fluid;
- has a transport function in the body, both taking nutrients to the cells and clearing waste products from them;
- aids in the regulation of body temperature;
- is a medium for chemical reactions.

Dehydration will not only affect the level of sports performance, but in the non-exercising state can leave you with a general sense of fatigue, headaches, a loss of appetite, or even feeling light-headed and nauseous.

On average, total daily fluid loss is approximately 2.6 litres. In order to maintain fluid balance, fluid intake should therefore meet this output. For a non-exercising individual it is recommended that a minimum of approximately 2 litres of fluid should be consumed per day, rising in warm weather and during exercise. The additional fluid required to maintain fluid balance will come from food and metabolism.

## Resting dietary composition

Once you know where the energy should come from, the key is to get the proportions correct. Scientific data suggest that resting energy

### PROMOTING FLUID INTAKE

- Drink before you get thirsty!
- Carry a bottle of water with you, and make a note of how many times it is refilled.
- Drink beverages you enjoy.
- Drink a glass of water with each meal.
- Eat plenty of fruit and vegetables with a high water content.
- Curb your consumption of beverages that have diuretic properties, such as caffeine.

requirements are approximately 42 per cent of energy from carbohydrate, 41 per cent from fat and 17 per cent from protein. Therefore, if energy is consumed in these ratios, and in appropriate quantities, it is sufficient to maintain

### HOW HYDRATED ARE YOU?

Clinically, hydration state is measured by assessing urinary specific gravity or urine osmolality. A simple test can see how many solutes your urine contains – essentially the concentration of your urine.

At home, the easiest assessment is to do the 'pee test'. In this, the first part of the urine stream is discarded, then ideally a small sample of urine is collected into a clear container. This should then be compared to a colour chart (see Figure 11.1). To put it simply, the darker the urine, the more dehydrated you are. A clear, or lightly coloured, sample is what you are hoping to produce. If not, you may need to review the amount of fluid you are consuming. Ideally, this should be under-taken first thing in the morning. However, such analysis can be undertaken to review and assess hydration during training practices.

Note, however, that certain medicines and vitamins may cause urine colour to change, and if any of these have been taken this test may be unreliable.

both health and a constant body weight for sedentary individuals.

Although these values differ from those proposed thus far, these intakes closely match those of the typical western diet of athletes and non-athletes alike (Blair *et al.*, 1981). However, getting the balance of nutrients correct is only a small part of the needs for the individual. An issue of far greater importance is correctly calculating required energy intake, hence the reason for the rise in body fat percentage for sedentary individuals and the increase in levels of obesity.

Thus far, only the needs for general nutrition have been considered. Once we consider the needs of the endurance athlete the proportions of energy required will change; these will be considered in chapter 11.

## Normal, 'healthy' diet

While we are sure many readers would love to be presented with a dietary plan to meet their 'ideal' needs for balance of nutrients and correct energy intakes, the key to achieving a 'healthy' and 'balanced' diet is variety.

The concept that some foods are 'bad' for you, while others are 'good', makes the whole complex interaction of the composition of food-stuffs oversimplified. Essentially, nutrients do not exist in isolation, and therefore are not eaten individually.

The key is to enjoy a wide variety of foods, both in each meal and in your general diet. The

Figure 9.1 An example of a food pyramid

widely available food pyramid (*see* Figure 9.1) thus acts as a good model for food use and variety, allowing you to choose plenty of what is good for you, but still enjoy a little of what may be considered to be less beneficial.

Most of your diet, as you will no doubt be already aware, should be made up of complex carbohydrates such as bread, cereals, rice, pasta and potatoes. Fresh fruit and vegetables will then not only provide additional sources of carbohydrate, but will also ensure the provision of essential vitamins and minerals.

Essential fats should preferably come from dairy produce, such as milk, eggs or yoghurt, while further fats and also protein will be obtained from fish, white meat, and beans or nuts. The sparing use of processed fats, oils and sweets is then advised.

# 10
# FUEL FOR SPORT

Having examined the dietary requirements for health and well-being, it is important to understand how these requirements may change for individuals involved with physical activity. Considering that a typical adult male of 80 kg (12 st 8 lb) and 15 per cent body fat will have the capacity to store carbohydrate in the muscle to a maximum of 300–400 g, and a total liver store of 80–100 g, this means that when the body is fully loaded with carbohydrate, at best it will have available 500 g of carbohydrate. With each 1 g of carbohydrate yielding just over 5 kcal of energy, the total energy available from carbohydrate is approximately 2000 kcal.

In comparison, the same individual will be carrying a total of 12 kg of fat, which equates to over 50 times the amount of energy as that stored within carbohydrate (115,000 kcal).

Looking at the example in table 10.1, even if that individual should lose a large proportion of their fat mass, and be carrying just 6 per cent body fat (the equivalent of a male elite endurance athlete), their total body mass would fall to 72.3 kg, with a drop of 7.7 kg of body fat, but they would still be storing around 40,000 kcal of energy as fat. This fat storage would rise by 10.7 kg and a total of 215,000 kcal, for someone carrying 25 per cent body fat.

## Energy efficiency

So with all this energy available from fat, why are the limited stores of carbohydrate of importance? Quite simply, the burning of fat as a fuel is a long, slow process, and does not yield as high an energy release as carbohydrate. Oxygen is needed to burn either fat or carbohydrate but, unfortunately, there is a limit to how

**Table 10.1 Percentage body fat, fat mass and energy available**

| Weight (kg) | % Body fat | Lean mass (kg) | Fat mass (kg) | Fat energy (kcal) |
|---|---|---|---|---|
| 72.3 | 6 | 68.0 | 4.3 | 40,000 |
| 80.0 | 15 | 68.0 | 12.0 | 115,000 |
| 90.7 | 25 | 68.0 | 22.7 | 215,000 |

much oxygen the body can take up and use. For an elite endurance athlete this can be as much as five to seven litres of oxygen every minute, but it is unlikely that much more than four litres of oxygen can be extracted from the air and used every minute during sustained exercise. For a typical club runner aiming to complete a marathon in around three hours 30 minutes, their maximal oxygen consumption is more likely to be around four litres per minute while running at 16–17 km/h, with the individual sustaining about three litres per minute, when running close to 12 km/h pace (depending on the efficiency of the individual's running style).

Given that, for each litre of oxygen the energy yield from fat is 4.686 kcal, and from carbohydrate it is 5.047, during high-intensity work, where the ability to consume oxygen is near its limit, the body will preferentially burn carbohydrate as it provides a greater amount of energy to move the body. The final twist to the release of energy is that, for each litre of oxygen used,

approximately 0.5 g of fat would be burned, whereas nearly 1.25 g of carbohydrate is utilised.

So, for every minute of exercise, the club-level runner consuming three litres of oxygen would be burning an estimated 3.75 g of carbohydrate. Even with a full carbohydrate store, this is enough to sustain just 133 minutes of exercise before the energy source is depleted and exercise has to slow or stop completely. This is the process that occurs when the runner 'hits the wall' and cannot maintain their pace. At this point muscle glycogen is at a point where the intensity cannot be sustained. In some cases, blood levels of carbohydrate (blood glucose) also fall very low, and reach a level where exercise cannot be continued at all, and in some very extreme cases full brain function cannot be sustained and collapse occurs.

This feeling of exhaustion is caused because although the body can utilise fat stores to keep you going, it can only supply a much smaller amount of energy from fat than it can from carbohydrate. This is an extreme situation; what happens before the body reaches this point is that fat is burned when exercising at a low intensity with the use of carbohydrate coming in as the intensity increases.

So if you are well trained and walking briskly or jogging very slowly on a flat route, it would be possible to sustain exercise for a very long duration as the fat would provide a large amount of the energy required (but not all the energy needed to sustain activity). However, if that same runner trains hard for 30–40 minutes, with a series of flat-out interval efforts, it would be possible for them to completely exhaust their carbohydrate store.

How much fat and carbohydrate you can utilise is dependent on the efficiency of your cardiovascular system, which is how efficient you become in getting oxygen to the muscle. The more oxygen you can get to the muscle per minute, the more able your body is to use fat as a fuel source before needing to dig in to its carbohydrate reserves. In a long-distance training session, or during a marathon or ultra-marathon, this is obviously a crucial factor. You want to be able to run as far as possible in using the greatest amount of fat metabolism, thereby saving your precious carbohydrate stores for the latter part of the race, or pacing so that fatigue hits just as you approach the finish line.

## Effect of diet

Despite the fact that exercise intensity and oxygen uptake have a major effect on the ability to sustain endurance exercise, this is not the only key factor in your ability to keep going on an endurance run. The level of dietary carbohydrate has a large impact on levels of muscle glycogen (the storage form of carbohydrate). In 1967 Bergstrom and his colleagues (Bergstrom et al., 1967) clearly demonstrated the effects of a low (5 per cent), moderate (40 per cent) and high (82 per cent) carbohydrate diet during cycling (see Figure 10.1). When these trained cyclists ate the low-carbohydrate diet, glycogen levels remained low and the riders could tolerate only moderate-intensity exercise for 60 minutes before fatigue, whereas with the high-carbohydrate intakes, muscle glycogen storage was high and cyclists exercised for over three hours before fatigue. There is no reason why this would be different for runners, and this is

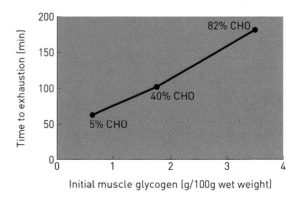

Figure 10.1 The impact of dietary carbohydrate percentage on muscle glycogen storage, and its relationship to time to exhaustion during exercise (Bergstrom et al., 1967 Acta Physiologica Scandinavica, Wiley-Blackwell Publishing)

one of many examples that shows the importance of high dietary carbohydrate for individuals undertaking exercise.

## Repeated-days training

Similarly, in 1980, Costill and Miller published scientific data which suggested that when well-trained runners undertook just an hour of moderate to intense exercise every day, it took only three days to empty a moderately full glycogen store when consuming a moderate carbohydrate intake (with carbohydrate supplying 45–50 per cent of the daily energy requirements), whereas if a high-carbohydrate diet (65–70 per cent of daily dietary requirements) was

consumed, the result was near full repletion of the glycogen stores to allow normal training on subsequent days (*see* Figure 10.2). More recently, Palmer *et al.* (1999) have shown that, with a high carbohydrate intake, competitive performance was maintained in three days of simulated competition, whereas large drops in performance occurred when only a moderate-carbohydrate diet was consumed.

These are but a few 'classic' studies. However, the overwhelming wealth of scientific data suggest that, to maintain optimal performance, sufficient levels of dietary carbohydrate need to be consumed. In terms of daily intake, 60–75

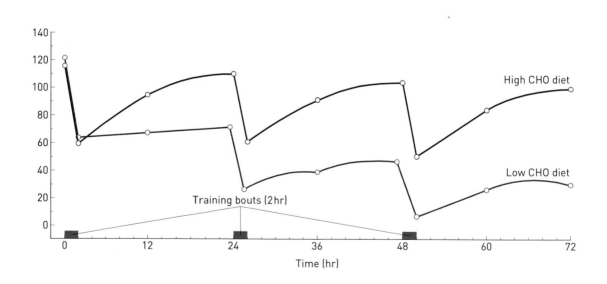

Figure 10.2 Costill and Miller (1980, International Journal of Sports Medicine) propose that a high-intake carbohydrate diet will more rapidly restore muscle glycogen when athletes undertake repeated days of training

per cent of energy should come from carbo-hydrates. This will ensure that carbohydrates burned during exercise are replaced daily. In order to compensate for differing body sizes, the intakes can be related to body mass. Target intake will be between 5 and 10 g of carbo-hydrate per kilogram of body mass. The actual need will be determined by the amount of exercise being undertaken (in terms of hours per day), the intensity of the exercise (the higher the intensity, the more carbohydrates are burned), and also the type of exercise (running, which is a weight-bearing exercise, requires a greater amount of energy than when cross-training and undertaking a non-weight-bearing exercise, such as swimming or cycling).

## Protein burning

In addition to the high need to provide the body with a constant supply of carbohydrate to provide the energy for activity, as highlighted earlier, carbohydrate has a protein-sparing role. This is particularly evident during training. Data from the early 1980s show that protein break-down significantly increases as a result of exercise, when compared to rest. This is not surprising, as part of training is to stimulate an increased growth of muscle fibre by causing minor breakdown. However, the most interesting factor from this research was that when comparing exercise during a high- and low-carbohydrate status, there was more than twice as much protein being broken down when dietary, and therefore muscular, carbohydrate levels were low. This is clearly illustrated in Figure 10.3 and re-emphasises the need for a

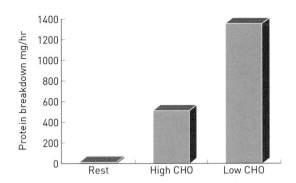

Figure 10.3 The impact of carbohydrate intake on protein turnover adapted from Lemon and Nagel, Medicine and Science in Sport and Exercise 13(3), (1981)

high-carbohydrate diet while training, and adequate protein intake.

## The importance of hydration

In addition to energy requirements, maintenance of hydration at rest and during exercise is vital to the performance of the body. One of the first things to happen when you start exercising is that your body temperature rises and you begin to sweat. Even in the depths of winter, you will be sweating to dissipate heat and keep your body temperature down. Individuals can lose more than three litres of fluid per hour when exercising in hot conditions. The fluid you lose reduces the blood volume, which places greater strain on your cardiovascular system, so your heart rate increases and the efficiency of oxygen delivery is reduced.

Sweating increases as exercise intensity increases (Brouns, 1991), so the harder you are working the more fluid you need to drink; conversely, the higher the relative exercise intensity, the more gastric emptying reduces (as will be discussed later). Recreational runners, or those with a higher percentage of body fat, will find it more difficult to dissipate heat and so will often sweat more. Smaller, lean runners will generally find it easier to cope with excessive heat than larger athletes, as they have a larger skin surface area when compared to their body mass so will be able to dissipate heat more quickly. A 1–2 per cent decrease in body weight due to sweat loss will result in performance being significantly reduced. So you can see how important it is for the endurance runner to be aware of dehydration.

# 11

# OPTIMAL NUTRITION FOR EXERCISE

Having provided some insight into the changes in metabolism and fuel utilisation from rest to exercise, and how it impacts on the body's ability to perform endurance exercise, in this chapter we will look at nutritional strategies before, during and after training to achieve optimal exercise. We will begin with the role nutrition plays in recovering from a training session. This may seem a back-to-front way of looking at it, but there is a valid reason for approaching it this way.

Primarily, many runners may struggle to follow the appropriate strategies before or during running, or may consider the duration of the event not to be greatly impacted by nutritional strategy. In these cases, recovery nutrition becomes even more vital. Second, but perhaps more importantly, recovery is the key to

optimising the benefits you get from training. Training is simply the stimulus the body requires to initiate its adaptation to cope with the increasing physical demands made upon it. Changes in muscle tissue, in the cardiovascular system and in the efficiency of your metabolism occur as a response to training (the recovery phase) and not during the training itself. Get your recovery right and you will be able to train harder and more frequently, which will mean more rapid improvements in fitness. Get your recovery wrong and you will soon find yourself fatigued!

## Nutrition for recovery

### Timing

As has been emphasised earlier, during exercise carbohydrates are the predominant fuel used by the body. Consider the example of a runner burning 225 grams of carbohydrate per hour during a steady endurance effort (that is, running using approximately three litres of oxygen every minute of exercise – *see* page 140). If they've done a one-hour training run, and taken carbohydrate drinks or gels during that session, they will have been able to replace only around 60 grams of carbohydrate. So, after just 60 minutes of training, they will already have a deficit of around 165 grams of carbohydrate.

While intake of carbohydrate pre-exercise may top up liver glycogen and blood glucose to ensure the best possible start to the training session or race, and carbohydrates during exercise will prolong exercise, as we will show later this will not be sufficient to meet all the demands of exercise. Therefore, following even a short training session or race of 10 km, or 10 miles (16.1 km), there will be a need to restore glycogen. This emphasises the importance of an appropriate recovery strategy.

Due to an increase in enzyme activity stimulated by exercise, following exercise there is a window of around two hours in which the body is better able to replenish its carbohydrate stores. So it is critical to start the recovery process as soon as possible after activity, ideally within 10–15 minutes of the session or event ending.

## Carbohydrate

The current scientifically based guidelines from the International Olympic Committee (2003) suggest that endurance athletes should aim to consume 1 gram of carbohydrate per kilo of body weight after training (approximately 50–100 g of carbohydrate, depending on body weight). This intake can be repeated hourly, possibly at frequent intervals, until the normal meal pattern is resumed. This is appropriate for a typical 90-minute to two-hour training session or race, but this strategy may need to be refined to take account of individual needs or different training sessions.

## Protein

In addition to carbohydrate, it may also be important to take on board some protein. Around 15–20 grams of protein, combined with the recommended amount of carbohydrate, may improve the rate at which muscle glycogen stores can be replaced, and it is also available to help to repair any muscle tissue damaged during exercise.

## Rehydration

Along with restoring your energy needs, you also need to make sure you replace water lost during exercise. You need to drink about 1.2–1.5 litres of fluid for each kilogram of weight lost. Therefore, if you have lost one kilogram of weight during your run, this equates to one litre of fluid (sweat) loss, and you need to drink around one and a quarter litres. If your body weight is down by two kilograms then you need to drink around two and a half to three litres. Of course, this fluid should be taken in gradually, at a comfortable rate. Once your body weight is back to normal you can return to drinking fluid normally.

In addition to replacement of fluid, replenishment of salts lost through sweating may also be required. Foods can usually replace all the salt that is needed, but some individuals find it difficult or impractical to eat immediately following exercise. In such cases, beverages containing electrolytes can be beneficial. Not only will the electrolyte content aid fluid uptake, but the addition of sodium and potassium in a drink will often increase its palatability, thereby encouraging the athlete to drink post-exercise.

## Sports recovery drinks

While you can consume solid food, and drink water, the easiest and most effective way of maximising your recovery is to use a sports

### TRAINING TIP: HOW LONG DOES IT TAKE YOU TO REHYDRATE?

Urine production is a great marker of your level of rehydration. Following training, make a note (mental or otherwise) of how long it is before you need to 'pee'. If you are well hydrated during your session, you should be ready to pass water fairly soon after the completion of your training. If you have not been drinking appropriately, it may take some time!

Urine colour will also act as a good indicator of your hydration status (see Figure 11.1).

Remember: your body needs to be well hydrated to function at its best, so rehydration is vital to optimal recovery.

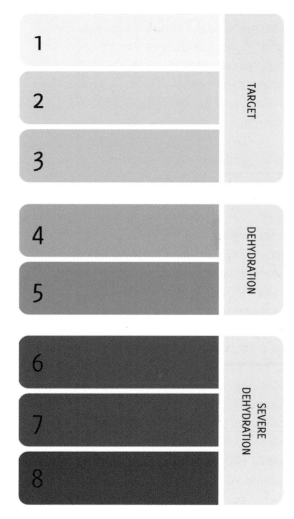

Figure 11.1 Urine colour chart commonly used to assess hydration status

recovery drink immediately following exercise, and then begin to eat normally within one to two hours post-exercise. There are many on the market, but it is important to use one of the products that is palatable and easy to transport to your training or competition venue. Powder forms that you mix with water are usually ideal.

There are some recovery drinks that are mixed with milk, but the addition of milk may slow down the rate at which the nutrients can be absorbed and so delay the recovery process. Care may also be needed when using milk-based products, in terms of total dietary fat intake.

Eating solid food is fine if there is no sports recovery drink available, but it may not be the preferred option as it can take several hours to digest solid food. For example, an unripe (green/yellow-skinned) banana will take up to four to six hours to be fully digested and its carbohydrate absorbed. If carbohydrate-rich foods are to be consumed, those with a moderate to high glycaemic index (GI) are preferred. Bread, fruit juices, sugar, jam, honey and breakfast cereals should all be adequate.

For individuals looking to exercise twice per day, a specifically formulated recovery drink is always the preferred option as it is the quickest way to supply your body with all the energy it needs. If you are expecting to have 24 hours or more recovery between training sessions, these issues are not as critical. In either case, the immediate post-exercise recovery should be followed, around two to three hours after training has been completed, by a normal meal.

## Nutrition prior to training

This is one of the most contentious areas of sports nutrition research. The guidelines of the IOC suggest that, if appropriate and adequate recovery nutrition has been applied and the athlete has taken sufficient care over 'resting'

### EATING FOR RECOVERY: KEY POINTS

- Approximately 1 g of carbohydrate per kg body weight within 15 minutes (e.g. 50–100 g)
- 15–20 g protein can assist in improving recovery rate
- Rehydrate at a comfortable rate to replace all sweat loss.

nutrition, pre-exercise nutrition should serve only to 'top up the tank'. However, studies of pre-exercise nutrition strategies have investigated different regimens where starting levels of muscle glycogen vary widely. There may also be significant variation in responses to different strategies between individuals. This makes the provision of a scientifically determined 'optimal' strategy nearly impossible.

For endurance training, as we have already seen, it is vital to ensure that the carbohydrate stores in the body are as replete as possible. The period prior to exercise is therefore critical to maximise and/or top-up glycogen stores.

### Pre-exercise carbohydrate intake

The current advice from the Medical Commission of the International Olympic Committee for preparation for endurance competition is to consume 1–4 grams of carbohydrate per kilogram of body weight in the six-hour period prior to exercise. Alternatively, they suggest when a carbohydrate loading strategy (*see* page 156) has been employed, if preferred, the athlete should consume no carbohydrate in the six hours pre-exercise. This gives a massive range recommended, from zero to 320 g (for an 80 kg individual), to be consumed in the six hours pre-exercise. The best advice that can realistically be given is to try a variety of strategies and find what works best for you, for that particular competitive situation, bearing in mind that, for shorter-distance events (10 km to 16 km), the necessity will not be so great as for longer races (over half-marathon distance) or training sessions.

### Three to four hours pre-training

In order to maximise carbohydrate stores you should have a high-carbohydrate meal three to four hours prior to training. This allows the body time to digest the majority of the food and clear the system before training commences.

### Two hours pre-training

If it is not possible to eat three to four hours pre-exercise, or if it feels appropriate to curb hunger, around two hours before exercise it may be a good idea to have a light carbohydrate snack containing about 50–80 grams of carbohydrate.

In practice, if you are training or racing first thing in the morning, neither of these options may be possible as it is probably not advisable to lose a couple of hours' sleep in order to have a pre-training meal. In this case, nutritional intake from solid food may be best avoided, or possibly substituted with an energy replace-ment drink. Again, you would be strongly advised to try this in training several times to investigate what works best, before applying the strategy in a key race and finding that something sits heavily on your stomach or, worse, causes diarrhoea!

### Within two hours of training

After this time, the research is equivocal as to further carbohydrate intake. Where muscle glycogen levels are not replete, further consumption of carbohydrate does not appear to have a marked impact on subsequent exercise metabolism. However, where carbohydrate stores are not completely full, intake of carbohydrate in the 30–60 minutes prior to exercise may elevate blood glucose and insulin. The resultant impact is that, during the first 30 minutes of exercise, carbohydrate metabolism is elevated and fat metabolism suppressed. In turn, this could potentially reduce the time to exhaust the carbohydrate stores and ultimately result in premature fatigue, especially in longer training sessions or races, or where no energy intake is consumed during exercise.

A further impact of consuming solid food within the final two hours prior to exercise is the potential gastric discomfort that could be caused if the food has not been fully digested or absorbed. It is therefore suggested that food is either avoided during this time, or at least that the athlete experiments to find a strategy that best fits their individual needs.

### Early-morning exercise

The practicalities discussed thus far suggest that while it may be possible to consume solid food prior to early-morning exercise, it may be better to have a good, high-carbohydrate meal the night before. If adequate time is available between waking and exercise it may be possible to consume 50–80 grams of carbohydrate. If this is not practical, then exercise can be commenced without the need for prior nutrition.

### Pre-exercise fluid ingestion

In addition to carbohydrate needs, the need for pre-exercise hydration should not be overlooked. If you are eating solid food two hours before training, then it is advisable to also have around 400–700 ml of fluid at the same time, so that you are properly hydrated before you commence training or racing, and yet allow for time for urination of excess fluid. Some athletes actually find it beneficial to avoid solid food intake at this time, and prefer to combine the required fluid load and consume the relevant carbohydrates with a sports drink.

### The final 15 minutes

For training sessions or races of longer than one hour, or where sweat loss may be heavy (for example, on a very warm, still day or when running on a treadmill) the final 10–15 minutes before you start exercising (or warming up pre-competition) can be used to provide a final top-up of fluid and fuel to the body.

A volume of 200–600 ml of fluid can be sipped gradually over this time. It should leave you feeling 'comfortably full', but not bloated. This intake of fluid will fill the stomach. During exercise, sports science research tells us that maintaining a steady flow of fluid to the stomach, and keeping it slightly stretched, will promote emptying to the intestine, and thereby fluid absorption. Hence the pre-exercise intake is the first stage in priming the body to better accept fluid and maintain hydration status. In the same way that a water tank in a house is constantly topped up when water is used for a shower, the body works better when a supply of water to the stomach is topped up too.

If you are consuming pre-exercise fluids, topping up your energy levels immediately prior to exercising is also wise. The inclusion of 20–40 g of carbohydrate means that, by the time your training session begins, this energy will just be reaching the blood and will be ready for use, but without creating an insulin response in the body, which could cause a dip in energy levels.

Going out training with a stomach comfortably full of fluid can take some getting used to if you haven't tried this method before. But it may be worth persevering with it, as it allows you to have the maximum amount of energy available for your training session, especially if you are looking to compete over marathon-type distances.

## Nutrition during training

As we have already seen, carbohydrate is the predominant fuel used during any form of

## PRE-EXERCISE NUTRITION: KEY POINTS

- 3–4 hours before: normal meal, containing between 50 and 200 g of carbohydrate
- Approximately 2 hours before: light snack containing 50–80 g carbohydrate, if required
- 30 minutes to 2 hours before: possibly avoid solid food intake
- Immediately prior to exercise (10–15 minutes pre-warm-up) 200–400 ml, 5–10 per cent (20–40 g) carbohydrate drink

exercise, and in particular it plays a key role in optimising performance during endurance exercise. So, when training, it is carbohydrate that must be replaced in order to enable the athlete to complete the training session effectively, and to make sure they recover as quickly as possible before the next training effort.

## Carbohydrate uptake

Despite carbohydrate oxidation rates in excess of 2–3 grams per minute, even with low-intensity training sessions, during exercise your body can process ingested energy at a rate of only about one gram of carbohydrate per minute. That is, it is only possible to get a maximum of about one gram of carbohydrate per minute from ingested drinks or gels to the working muscle.

As a general rule it is advisable to scale this to match your body size, and take in one gram per kilogram of body weight for every hour of the training. For example, an 80 kg runner would consume approximately 80 grams of carbohydrate for each hour of training they were undertaking. In order to provide a constant source of energy, this means consuming carbohydrate on a regular basis, perhaps sipping a carbohydrate drink every 5–10 minutes – not waiting until 60 minutes into your session and gulping down a bottle of energy drink! Little and often is the key.

## Solid or liquid?

During longer training sessions or races some runners prefer to consume solid food (such as jelly babies or pieces of fruit) to deliver their energy requirements. Scientific evidence suggests that the energy yield from solids can be as beneficial as from gels or fluids. However, the key choice that the individual should make when deciding the most appropriate strategy is whether the energy form will empty from the stomach rapidly, and if it is likely to cause any gastro-intestinal disturbances such as discomfort, bloating, or even vomiting or diarrhoea.

Solid foods will often take longer to empty from the stomach than fluids, particularly as they may also contain fat and dietary fibre. This can in turn increase the possibility of a stomach upset, or suppress required fluid consumption due to a 'full' feeling. However, as solid foods may be more portable and very concentrated, they can often be of benefit when undertaking a very long event, such as an ultra-marathon, by alleviating a hungry or empty feeling.

As with many of the nutritional practices discussed here, the key is to determine a strategy that works for you, for a variety of different exercise intensities, durations and climatic conditions.

### Less than an hour

For a training session of less than one hour some carbohydrate intake may be beneficial. It is unlikely that you will exhaust your carbohydrate store in under an hour unless you undertake a really hard interval session. On the other hand, we have to constantly be aware of the strategy of training and recovering.

If you feed during a training session that lasts one hour or less, you will have started to replenish the carbohydrate that you are burning. While it is unlikely that you will finish the training session in an 'energy neutral' situation – that is to say, you have virtually the same amount of

## GELS

Sports gels are a concentrated form of energy for the athlete to use while exercising. Being semi-liquid in form they are easier to consume than solid food (which can break into small pieces and cause choking while running) and also reduce the need to carry a large bottle when carbohydrate needs are prioritised over hydration. As such they are often the preferred choice of many runners to meet carbohydrate needs during longer training runs and races, and can also be used in shorter events where a boost of energy may be welcomed.

Sports energy gels are made by a large number of manufacturers in packaging designed to be easy to carry, simple to open and easy to consume. A wide variety of flavours means they should be agreeable to most palates.

However, as a word of warning, while gels come in a variety of volumes and concentrations, they do not meet your hydration needs. Therefore you must make sure you drink appropriately. Some gels recommend consumption of 500 ml of water at the same time as consuming the gel, while others are isotonic and don't need water to be taken when they are consumed, but still require the athlete to drink to avoid dehydration.

Finally, if you choose to use a gel, make sure you find it agreeable before you first try it on a race day; the concentrated carbohydrate could cause gastric discomfort. Also make sure you know how many gels you need to meet your specific energy requirements.

## HOW MUCH TO DRINK

It may be important to assess how much you sweat, in order to calculate how much to drink, for both winter and summer training. Here's the easy way to do it.

- Jump on the scales (preferably naked) before you train, remembering to keep a note of your weight. (Don't forget to get dressed before you go training or you may get arrested!)
- Enjoy your session, and drink as you normally would. Recording your fluid intake (mentally or otherwise) can also be of use to help calculate your sweat rate.
- Weigh yourself as soon after the training session as possible (naked and towelled dry).
- Any difference in body mass is sweat loss that you have not replaced. Every 0.5 kg lost equals 500 ml fluid. (You may be surprised how much you sweat, even in winter.)
- Add the body mass lost to volume consumed; this equals total sweat loss. To calculate sweat rate, divide the total amount by the time of the training session. This will give you an idea of fluid needed for the intensity, duration and weather conditions in future sessions.
- Finally, the chances are you have not fully hydrated during your training session, so in order to fully rehydrate, drink 1.25 times the volume of weight lost.

carbohydrate stored in the body at the end of training as you did at the beginning, the amount of glycogen that will need to be replenished will be less. This means you should recover faster, ready for the next session.

## Fluid needs

As we have already seen, sweat losses during exercise can vary widely due to environmental conditions and exercise intensity. In order to avoid the adverse effects of dehydration it is key to replenish as much of the fluid loss as is practical. Scientific evidence suggests that, while running, it may be possible to absorb as much as 0.8 to 1.0 litres of fluid per hour, this

## WATER: TOO MUCH OF A BAD THING?

*Hyponatraemia* is medically defined as a low plasma sodium. It can occur in endurance runners when excess water has been consumed or when there is a significant loss of sodium (through sweat loss), or a combination of both, to the extent that the salts in the body have been diluted to a lower than desirable level. Symptoms include nausea, headaches, bloating and, in the most severe cases, death.

**Figure 11.2 The importance of fluid intake during distance running must not be overlooked**

however is reduced as exercise intensity increases. Ideally, it is best to finish a training session with minimal dehydration, in order to maintain optimal performance and decrease recovery time.

During training and racing, fluid intake should be prioritised, and drinking should start soon

after the training session commences. The key to maintaining hydration status is then to keep drinking small amounts on a regular basis. It appears that gastric emptying of sports drinks consumed during exercise is best promoted by maintaining a volume of liquid in the stomach, in just the same way the water storage unit in the roof space of a house is kept topped up to maintain the water pressure at the taps. Therefore it is advisable to drink every 10–15 minutes. The volume of each drink should be targeted to match your expected sweat loss for the conditions and intensity of the training effort.

## Nutrition for training camps

This section gives advice on those wanting to train day after day with no rest days in between. It's a situation you may find yourself in if you choose to take part in a training camp. The advice here will also apply to anyone attempting to participate in multiple-day races

### NUTRITIONAL STRATEGY DURING EXERCISE: KEY POINTS

- Small, regular feedings of carbo-hydrate (up to 1 g of carbohydrate per kg body mass per hour)
- Moderate concentration/appropriate fluid balance (to replace sweat loss)
- Ideally around 100–150 ml of fluid containing a 5–10 per cent carbo-hydrate solution every 10–15 minutes.

such as the Guernsey Easter Runs or Horwich Carnival Races.

Elite or competitive distance runners preparing for a spring marathon will often go on a training camp early in the year. Many of these camps are held in the warmer climes of southern Europe or the isles of north Africa, and are great if you come from northern Europe and have to struggle to do longer or more intense training sessions in the early part of the year when the weather is cold and wet. A week or so in Majorca, southern France or Lanzarote offers warmer weather and access to some different terrain to that available at home. So camps are a good way to supplement your training if you have the time and funds to do them.

However, there is a word of warning. It is common for runners to go to these training camps and get carried away with the experience. On a training camp you will usually be training with a lot of other keen club athletes, all eager to make the most of the warm weather and time available. This will usually mean training a lot harder on consecutive days than you would have done had you stayed at home. That's a good thing as it helps motivation, but it also means that recovering after each session becomes even more important. A runner on a training camp doing up to three sessions per day on consecu-tive days may need as much as 500 to 800 grams of carbohydrate per day if they are to recover adequately. This will mean a massive increase in solid food intake, which for most people is simply not practical – or palatable.

In such cases, the solution is to supplement the normal dietary intake with high-carbohydrate energy drinks and snacks. In addition to the normal eating pattern, carbohydrate should be consumed in small amounts at regular intervals, both during and following training. The use and timing of recovery products is also vital for this sort of training.

One of the major issues surrounding such heavy days of repeated exercise is that athletes can suffer from poor sleep, sore muscles, a feeling of restless or heavy legs, mood swings and hormonal imbalances. Immune system function can also be suppressed. These are all classic symptoms of over-training. This can often be seen when returning from the training camp – with the additional stresses of air travel, athletes come down with minor illnesses such as sore throats, coughs or colds.

## Race-day nutrition

Ideally, your race-day nutrition strategy should begin a few days prior to your chosen event. Carbohydrate loading is something that has received a lot of publicity over the years, particularly in relation to marathon running. Years ago marathon runners would drastically reduce their carbohydrate intake two weeks before a race while continuing to train as normal. After a week on this regime the runner's stores of glycogen would be completely exhausted, as would the runner! A week before the race the athlete would then load up on a high-carbohydrate diet right up to race day.

The theory was that the carbohydrate starvation process would cause the body to crave carbohydrates so that, when a high-carbohydrate diet was introduced after a week, it would result in a significant increase in the amount of carbohydrate that could be stored. This would, in theory, mean that more glycogen would be available for use in the race.

More recent research suggests that there is no significant gain to be had from carbohydrate loading in this way. It is much better to simply increase your carbohydrate intake in the week before a race while reducing the training load. This has the same effect as the old-fashioned carbohydrate loading method, but without the negative effects of the athlete feeling run-down and lethargic for a week, and struggling to maintain any meaningful training regime due to a lack of available energy.

So, in the week before a race, reduce the training load and gradually increase your carbohydrate intake from the normal intake by approximately 1–2 grams per kilo of body weight per day. In the final two to three days pre-event, you should aim to increase your daily carbohydrate intake to 8–10 grams per kilo of body weight per day. By doing this, the muscles 'supercompensate' – that is, they become loaded with a much higher level of glycogen than normal.

There are, however, some drawbacks to be aware of. You are likely to feel very heavy legged in the few days prior to the race and at the start of the event. This is due to increased water absorption caused by the increased glycogen levels in the muscle. This is a perfectly normal sensation, but it is worth putting up with as it means that you go into the race with as much carbohydrate on board as possible.

Care must also be taken with regard to the source and timing of carbohydrate loading. If large amounts of fructose (fruit sugars) are consumed, or large amounts of carbohydrate consumed at any one time, the body may struggle to absorb all the carbohydrate introduced. If this then reaches the lower intestine, the bacteria will have a field day and the most likely result is diarrhoea. Not ideal as pre-race preparation!

Carbohydrate loading would also not be recommended for the shorter distance races because of these negative aspects, and would generally only be suggested for events where the athlete is likely to be exercising for longer than two hours.

## During the race

In races of up to half-marathon distance, you may be best served by optimising your pre-race nutrition, and then taking water and energy drink or gels where you are able. However, for races longer than this, getting enough energy and fluid on board is crucial if you are to perform at your best on race day. Remember, solid foods may take longer to digest than food in liquid or gel form, and while you may be happy to eat jelly beans during training, the slightly increased intensity at race pace, may cause problems with gastric emptying.

It is perfectly possible to take on board enough energy for an event of several hours' duration by using energy drinks and gels. However, some individuals will find this difficult. As mentioned previously, as your exercise intensity increases, gastric emptying

## CARBOHYDRATE LOADING: KEY ISSUES

- Reduce your training load over the final week.
- Gradually increase dietary carbohydrates.
- In the final two to three days, carbohydrate intake should reach 8–10 g per kg body mass.
- Carbohydrate loading may cause unwelcome side effects.
- Carbohydrate loading would be recommended only for events of over two hours' duration.

shuts down, and this can leave you bloated and uncomfortable. You will need to constantly assess your need to drink in terms of replacing sweat loss from both exercise intensity and weather conditions, and balance this need against staving off dehydration and replenishing vital energy.

Unfortunately everyone responds differently, so experience is the key. Get it right and have the race of your life – get it wrong and the last miles can be agony!

## Issues with travel

Many races you undertake won't be taking place on your doorstep. It is very important to consider issues to do with travelling that may affect you. Clearly an 'overnight' to do a half marathon 100 or so miles from home is not going to have the same impact as travelling to do a major event like the New York Marathon. However, travelling to a race may present you with challenges to your nutrition, so it is best to plan ahead. Ideally, you want everything to be as normal as possible. Just because you are in France to run the Paris Marathon, doesn't mean your pre-race meal has to be frogs' legs!

The main challenges you are likely to face are the disruption to your normal routine, the lack of availability of 'tried and tested' or familiar foods, and the often inflexible pattern of mealtimes imposed by the opening hours of your hotel or local restaurants. Runners taking part in the London Marathon often note that, unless they are staying in an 'official' hotel, it is difficult to find breakfast with such an early start and the travel needed just to get to the start line. So why not plan ahead, and take some breakfast cereal with you? Additionally, having a supply of spreads, such as jam or honey, some sports bars, dried fruits and powdered energy drinks or liquid meal supplements may mean that all you need to source at your destination

## TRAINING TIPS: RACE STRATEGY

It is always very wise to determine, and then practise, your nutritional strategy prior to race day. Therefore have a number of nutritional strategies planned to accommodate the various weather conditions you may encounter (heat, cold and humidity) and for the distance of the event. On the morning of the big day (or the evening of the previous day if it is an early start) choose the most appropriate and try to stick to it.

Your strategy should focus on the following elements:

- **What to consume and when** This should take into account what you are able to carry with you and what is available at feed stations. You should be comfortable in the knowledge that any products you consume during the event agree with you. Never try something new on race day. If necessary, find out what energy drink or gels are provided, get a small supply and train with it (at race effort) to make sure you don't get any gastric disturbance. Similarly, just because supporters in the crowd are handing out slices of fruit, doesn't mean it will agree with you.
- **When to eat and drink** Timing of fluid and energy intake should be, as we have suggested, at regular intervals. But you also need to be flexible in that approach. Drinking every 10 minutes is a great way to remain hydrated, but may be rather difficult in a busy city marathon, or not needed on a cold, wet day.

Plan your strategy to take account of difficult sections of the race and the location of feed stations – and, remember, don't get caught up in the atmosphere and miss your planned early intake, as you may come to regret it towards the end of the event.

is water. This can take the stress out of a situation where you may arrive at a destination in the middle of the night, following a travel delay, and have to race the following morning.

## Putting it all into practice

So, now you know what you should be doing to prepare for and recover from training, but how do you put it into practice when work and

personal commitments get in the way? For example, if you have to train at 6 am before going to work, it may not be practical to get up at 4 am and have a meal before going training.

In this situation taking a carbohydrate energy drink immediately before you train may be the better option, and then follow the usual guidelines for nutrition during training and make sure you have a recovery drink after your training session. In this scenario having a good meal the previous evening is also a good idea in order to provide the energy you require first thing the next morning. Similarly, if you have to train after work you may not be back at home until 8 or 9 pm, meaning that your post-exercise meal would be consumed at around 11 pm or later. In this case, it may be better to have your normal recovery drink immediately after training and a light snack half an hour or so later, and to avoid a large meal. On days when training will take place later in the day, it is better to have a big breakfast, moderate lunch and maybe a late-afternoon snack to keep up your energy levels. The key, as with all nutritional strategies, is to find what works best for your particular circumstances.

# 12

# NUTRITIONAL TARGETS

## Assessing your needs

You should now know what and when to eat, but how much should you be eating? There are two keys targets for runners: the first is to replenish the energy used for daily activity and training, while maintaining body weight; the second aim for some athletes is to achieve optimal body weight and lose body fat for either health or performance benefits. Essentially, with the exception of some minor tweaks, the strategy for both objectives is the same, the only difference being the current body fat in relation to the desired body fat target.

## Assessing body composition

It is advantageous to assess body composition as part of a physiological analysis of any athlete. For a competitive runner facing a hilly race, or an event where changes in pace are likely to be needed (a cross-country event, for example), it is especially important to work out if they are carrying excess body fat. As running is a weight-bearing sport, performance will be hampered even on a flat course if you are carrying excess body fat.

Many sports science facilities will use special body fat callipers to measure skin-fold thickness at various points around the body. These measurements relate to the amount of subcutaneous fat. A number of theoretical formulae are then applied to the values to work out total body fat percentage. While many people like to know their body fat percentage, the sum of the skin-fold values is now being used more frequently, as this will show small changes in body composition with dietary intervention and training. This is considered one of the more practical, cost-effective and accurate ways of assessing body fat, and these methods are used by coaches and physiologists at the elite level in many sports worldwide. As an ideal, a well-trained athlete would be looking for the sum of seven sites to be between 40 and 60 mm, while an elite endurance athlete is likely to be targeting around 25–40 mm.

If you are not able to undergo such a test, there are ways of making an assessment of your body fat percentage, although it may not be as accurate as a proper physiological test. It is also worth pointing out that most of us will have at least some fat we can safely lose, and most of us can tell by jumping up and down in front of a mirror (semi-naked) or by pinching a bit of fat around our waistline whether we have fat to lose or not.

If you are not able to get a reliable method of skin-fold analysis, a measure of bioimpedance is cheap and widely available. Many chemists

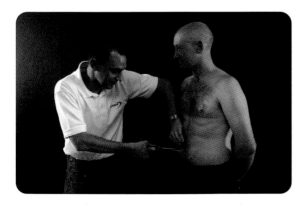

**Figure 12.1 An athlete undergoing body fat analysis using skin-fold callipers**

and sports retailers now sell scales that 'measure' body fat. These systems work by sending a small electric current through the body. This current will pass through muscle and fat at different speeds, and by measuring how long it takes to pass through the body, the scales work out the ratio of muscle to fat. As they do not take into account your levels of hydration (particularly as different levels of fluid can be stored in and around the cells) these systems can be inaccurate, and vary widely according to hydration status and the time of day the measurement is taken. However, even if the actual initial body fat figure is out it will always be out, so you will be able to see if your body fat percentage is dropping over weeks and months of training, so long as you always measure at the same time of day and under the same conditions (for example, first thing in the morning, following a rest day, after a visit to the bathroom).

Certainly bioimpedance scales are a better way of assessing body composition than the BMI (body mass index) system. This is often used as a way of working out if someone is overweight. It works by comparing an individual's weight and height. The result it produces is then compared to a table indicating whether someone is of normal weight, overweight or obese. The problem is that this method takes no account of whether someone has a muscular physique – it only uses a person's weight. So, a heavily muscled, very lean elite athlete can have a BMI that would class them as clinically obese.

## Body fat targets

Once you have an idea of your current body fat, it is worth looking at how this relates to other athletes. This is a relatively easy principle for male athletes, and classifications of body fat percentage can easily be found. An example of one classification is highlighted in table 12.1. In this example, the difference in fat mass and lean body mass is given for a 'typical' 80 kg male. As the table shows, an individual with the body fat percentage of an elite endurance athlete is likely to be carrying almost 20 kg less fat than someone who is 'morbidly obese' – that is half the weight of an elite female runner! Sadly, in the current climate, more males are over 30 per cent body fat; this includes some who exercise on a regular basis and successfully complete distance running events!

Similarly, the same comparison suggests that if those athletes were the same weight, the elite individual would have 20 kg more lean body mass. This would mostly be muscle mass, and is likely to be the reason that

| Table 12.1 Target body fat for male athletes | | | |
|---|---|---|---|
| Body fat percentage | Classification | Approximate fat mass of 80 kg individual | Approximate lean mass of 80 kg individual |
| 4–6% | Elite endurance athlete | 4 | 76 |
| 8–10% | Ideal 'competitive' athlete | 7 | 73 |
| 12–15% | Ideal normal population | 11 | 69 |
| 15–18% | Average normal population | 13 | 67 |
| 18–24% | Overweight | 17 | 63 |
| 24–30% | Medically at risk | 22 | 58 |
| 30%+ | Morbidly obese | 24 | 56 |

athletes in other sports can produce an exceptional amount of power. However, most elite male athletes not only have low body fat, but also are leaner and typically would weigh around 60 kg, have 56.6 kg lean mass and just 2.4 kg of fat mass.

Females, by their genetic composition, have naturally higher body fat levels than their male counterparts. The provision of specific classifications is also somewhat controversial. The 'ideal' target body fat for an athletic female is often considered to be in the region of 15–18 per cent, and lean considered to be around 18–22 per cent. Many elite females have had their body fat values recorded in single figures, but most are more likely to be around 10–12 per cent. Unfortunately, unless dietary intakes are absolutely on target, menstrual disturbances are often observed when body fat drops below 18 per cent. Therefore, the main focus when targeting an ideal body fat value for a female should be the maintenance of menstrual function, and therefore we suggest the minimum target for non-elite females should be 18 per cent.

Knowing your current body fat, and having an idea of a sensible target for your performance level, will give you an idea of how much weight it will be possible to lose. Certainly, in longer or hilly races, this will have a major impact on your performance ability. For example, the 80 kg individual, who is well within the range of the average population at 16.3 per cent body fat, would be carrying 13 kg of fat. If he was able to reduce his body fat to 10 per cent, and still

maintain the same lean body mass, he would reduce his fat mass and total mass by 5 kg.

The implications of this for predicted performance are vast. Let's assume our typical 80 kg runner has an absolute $VO_2$max of 4.0 L/min, and this does not change as a result of the weight loss. His relative $VO_2$max would increase from 50.0 ml/kg/min to 53.33 ml/kg/min, solely as a result of the decrease in fat mass. Using research by Daniels and Gilbert (1979) the predicted time for a marathon would drop from three hours 10 minutes and 40 seconds to three hours zero minutes and 33 seconds – a massive improvement in performance time of over 10 minutes, achieved through weight loss alone. Combine that with improvements in fitness through training, and the effects are significant.

## Keeping a diet diary

Many athletes keep a training diary, but if you are going to improve your nutrition it is equally important to keep a record of what you are eating. You don't have to do it every day, but you do need to do it for at least one week to work out what your diet consists of right now.

In the longer term it is useful to keep a record of your diet in the run-up to a major race so that you can determine what works for you and what doesn't. However, in the initial phase of your training, you need to determine how much energy you require to cope with the training programme you are undertaking. If you need to lose weight then it is a simple matter of making sure that the number of calories you take in is slightly under the number you are burning up.

It really is as simple as that, but getting the numbers right is crucial. If you reduce your calorie intake by too much you will impair your ability to train, and may cause your metabolism to slow down so much that it becomes impossible to lose weight at all. On extremely low-calorie diets your body will switch into a kind of 'hibernation' mode where more of the food you ingest is stored as fat than it normally would be. This is, of course, the exact opposite of what you are trying to achieve.

## Calculating your needs

The first stage in calculating your specific energy requirements is to estimate your resting metabolic rate. Resting metabolic rate is the energy that the body requires during complete rest in order to sustain basic life function. Although it is possible to measure this under very controlled clinical conditions, predictive calculations for resting metabolic rate dependent on age and gender will give you a good starting point (*see* table 12.2).

The next stage is to use the predicted resting metabolic rate to calculate daily energy expenditure. Daily energy expenditure is the energy needed to sustain the body through its daily activity, while remaining in a neutral energy balance – that is, without gaining or losing weight. Daily energy expenditure is calculated according to activity level throughout the day (*see* table 12.3). Some calculators of this incorporate physical training, however this will be added on later.

Most individuals fall into the classification of a 'light lifestyle' if they have predominantly inactive, office-based jobs that require little or no manual work. However, be aware that moving around the office, using the stairs, walking around the shops, or performing other

### Table 12.2 Prediction of resting metabolic rate

| Age | Up to 18 years old | 18–30 years old | Over 30 years old |
| --- | --- | --- | --- |
| Male | (W×17.5) + 651 | (W×15.3) + 679 | (W×11.6) + 879 |
| Female | (W×12.2) + 746 | (W×14.7) + 496 | (W×8.7) + 829 |

W = current body weight in kilograms
For example, a 45-year-old male of 80 kg would multiply his current weight by 11.6, then add 879 to this total, giving a predicted resting metabolic rate of 1807 kcal per day.

**Table 12.3 Calculation of daily energy expenditure**

| Lifestyle | Light | Moderate | Heavy |
|---|---|---|---|
| | RMR × 1.4 | RMR × 1.7 | RMR × 2.1 |

RMR = estimated resting metabolic rate.
For example, the 80 kg male with a resting metabolic rate of 1807 kcal, and a light lifestyle, would require approximately 2530 kcal per day.

daily tasks such as cooking or cleaning will not increase the energy required if you use this calculation. Someone with a very physical job, undertaking a large amount of manual labour, which means they have an increased heart rate and sweat rate for a predominant part of the working day, is more likely to be classified as having a 'heavy lifestyle'.

## Your sporting requirements

In order to truly calculate your energy requirements, you also need to calculate the energy expenditure from your training. This is where things become increasingly tricky. As a good starting point, estimated energy expenditure for running can be calculated as follows:

$$\text{Energy (kcal) per minute} = 0.1773 \times \text{Weight} + 0.0433$$

For the example of our 80 kg athlete, this would equal approximately 14.2 kcal per minute of running, or around 850 kcal per hour of training.

Again, using this equation, the importance of a reduced weight during running becomes apparent. A reduction in body mass of 5 kilograms would mean a reduction in energy expenditure of 50 kcal per hour – not a huge amount in a one-hour training session, but equivalent to needing another 44 g of carbohydrate during a three-and-a-half-hour marathon.

However, there is a problem with this formula: it is only an estimation. It is based on the assumption that a runner is averaging 12 kilometres per hour, on a flat road, as a solo effort, with no impact from head or tail winds. The calculation takes no account of terrain (particularly the amount of time spent running uphill or the severity of a climb); no account of environmental conditions (wind speed and direction in relation to the runner, or temperature); no account of road surface or conditions underfoot; and no account of maintenance of a constant pace. Therefore it can only be used as a starting point.

Similar formulae are available for different running paces, other sporting activities (cycling, gym work, etc.) and even household chores (like washing-up or cleaning the car). However, remember that, at best, these are only predictors, and could be wildly inaccurate depending on a host of factors, such as technique and efficiency.

Ideally, each training session should be monitored for intensity using heart rate, and possibly pace and climbing using GPS data, which can then be related back to the individual's measured maximum heart rate, resting heart rate, threshold levels, maximal oxygen consumption and running economy to accurately calculate the energy used in each training session.

### Your daily requirements

In order to calculate your daily energy requirement for training, you need to work out your calorie expenditure for a 'typical' training week. This should then be divided by seven days to give your average daily need. For example, if our 80 kg athlete does six hours of training per week, this would equal:

> 6 hours @ 850 per hour = 5100 kcal per week *or* 730 kcal per day (on average)

This daily training requirement should be added to the daily energy requirement. For example:

> Daily energy expenditure + daily average training requirements = total energy intake: 2530 + 730 = 3260 kcal

Therefore, this individual would need to consume an estimated total of 3260 kcal per day to provide all the energy needs for the body to maintain health, and allow for growth and repair, and also to replenish energy stores following training.

## Weight loss: a balancing act

Thus far, the energy calculations performed have been related to someone looking to maintain their natural body weight and be able to recover fully from training. So what changes need to be made for the individual who is looking to lose fat mass?

Quite simply, nutrition is a balancing act. If an individual is looking to maintain their current weight, energy intake must equal energy expenditure. Where they are looking to lose weight, energy intake should be lower than energy expenditure. The problem is, by how much?

Many runners wanting to lose weight believe that continuing to train while cutting out all the

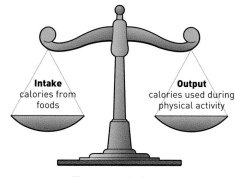

**The energy balance**

**Figure 12.2 Weight loss: a balancing act**

carbohydrate from their diet will cause them to burn more fat. Remember, this is not the case. Carbohydrate has to be present in order to burn fat as a fuel.

Another consequence of low-carbohydrate diets is that the body will use protein from muscle as a fuel if there is not enough carbohydrate available. So, if you've been on a long training session and run out of carbohydrate, the body will strip protein from muscle to provide energy, even though it is a much slower process.

This is why athletes on low-carbohydrate diets will often suffer severe muscle soreness and fatigue following hard training sessions. In extreme cases endurance athletes have suffered heart problems as a result of being on low-carbohydrate diets for extended periods. When the body strips protein from muscle it cannot differentiate between muscle types, so cardiac muscle may be utilised. All this emphasises the need for endurance athletes to maintain high levels of carbohydrate in their diet to produce not just optimum performance in training and racing, but also to promote general health. It cannot be emphasised enough how important it is to get the energy balance right for both exercise recovery and weight loss. Therefore, in order to successfully achieve weight loss, the energy balance must be delicately tilted. Although the press may publish fantastic celebrity diets, advocating the consumption of just 1500–2000 kcal per day, this is not enough to sustain daily training and promote successful fat loss. The key is to take

things slowly. The spare tyre round your waist didn't appear overnight – and unfortunately it won't vanish overnight either!

So, it's back to the calculation of daily requirements. For the athlete looking to maintain weight, the targets set should replenish all the energy expended and the body should remain in static balance. For the athlete looking to lose weight, a reduction in total calories of no more than 15 per cent should be undertaken. For our example athlete on 3260 kcal per day, this equates to a reduction in energy of 489 kcal per day. In this way, a slow, steady reduction of fat mass should be able to occur. Ideally, each week total body weight should drop by approximately 0.4 kg (1 lb). By ensuring this is undertaken with the correct balance of nutrients, you should preserve muscle mass, fully restore daily carbohydrate stores, maintain body water and lose only fat mass. Although greater reductions in energy may be tempting to achieve more rapid results, these often leave athletes tired, poorly recovered and, once back on a 'normal' eating strategy, back to the same, or even an increased, body weight.

If you try reducing your daily calorific total by 15 per cent and this leaves you with too little energy, try adjusting your diet until the calorific deficit is just 5 or 10 per cent, using the same calculation process. Stick to this total until you reach your target weight, then begin to consume the appropriate daily calorific total for your weight.

**Table 12.4 An example of dietary balance for training**

|  | g per kg per day | g | % of total energy | kcal |
|---|---|---|---|---|
| Target carbohydrate | 6.6 | 530 | 65 | 2119 |
| Target protein | 1.4 | 112 | 13.7 | 448 |
| Target fat |  | 77 | 21.3 | 693 |
| **Total energy** |  |  |  | 3260 |

## Energy balance

You now have a daily calorific total, but we now need to work out how much of those calories should come in the form of carbohydrate, how much from protein and how much from fat. A review of earlier chapters will remind you that, ideally, you should be aiming for around 60–75 per cent of calorific total as carbohydrate. You should then aim to consume 12–15 per cent of your daily energy requirement as protein. The remainder of your calorie total will be in the form of fat. An example of this can be seen in table 12.4.

In order to undertake these calculations, first divide your total energy into the carbohydrate percentage you are trying to achieve. For this example, 65 per cent of 3260 kcal is 2119 kcal. Next, to convert the calorific value to grams of carbohydrate, divide by 4 (this same calculation works for protein too): for example, 2119/4 = 530 g of carbohydrate. The same calculation can then be undertaken for protein required. To calculate the total fat allowance, the energy value needs to be divided by 9, in this example resulting in a daily allowance of 77 g of fat per day.

At this point, it is back to the diet diary to see what you are currently consuming, and where improvements can be made.

### Best practice

Unfortunately, simply eating the correct balance of nutrients won't bring the results you are looking for. For example, your nutritional balance could be spot on, but if you consumed all your daily calories in one sitting, the body would not be able to cope: carbohydrate storage would be incomplete, the body would not be able to process the large amount of protein, and excess energy would be converted and stored as fat. In this way, you would never be able to achieve the body composition you were aiming for. Best practice must therefore be followed wherever possible.

Ideally, you should look to eat smaller amounts on a regular basis. Some nutritional practitioners even suggest having five or six smaller meals a day. This allows for a steady flow of energy to the body, avoiding any highs and lows, and means the energy can be processed and stored at a sensible rate. Similarly, current thinking is also that the body cannot optimally tolerate any more than 25–30 g of protein per serving. Therefore, look to spread your protein needs throughout the day, if at all possible.

Consider eating what you want when you want, and also eat slowly and enjoy your food. This may sound dangerous, but if you eat when you are hungry, you will provide the body with the energy it needs, when it needs it. Also, if you eat slowly, taking time to savour and enjoy what you are eating, the body has time to recognise that you are providing it with energy and will give you plenty of notice when you have replenished sufficient needs. In the same way, avoid getting overly hungry. In this situation many people rush their food and overeat. If the stomach gets used to being 'overly full' your body will not so easily recognise the signs that

you have actually consumed sufficient amounts of energy.

Finally, avoid consuming a large amount of energy late in the evening (this includes the energy from your favourite alcoholic tipple!). Your metabolic rate slows as the day goes on, and a large meal late in the day may not be fully absorbed due to this slowing in metabolic rate. Excess calories will then be converted and stored as fat, again making it hard to recover or achieve fat mass targets. If you do find you have to train late in the day, a post-exercise snack should still be consumed, but best practice would be to 'front load' the day with your nutritional needs.

As with the rest of the advice in this book, these are just the guidelines you need to get you started. Everyone is different, and therefore no two strategies will give exactly the same results in different individuals. You will need to modify our advice to see what is most beneficial for your training, lifestyle and body. Continually review how things are progressing, and you will undoubtedly find what works best for you and will gain the greatest improvements.

# 5

# RACE DAY

# 13

# PUTTING IT ALL TOGETHER

This is it. After months of training, the big day is here. But the final preparations for your race begin long before you actually get to the start line. Taking some time a few weeks before the race to get your planning and preparation done is well worthwhile. There's little point in training for months for an event only to see your race ruined by something you have forgotten to pack, or because your travel plans have not been sorted out. Remember the five Ps: **P**oor **P**lanning leads to **P**athetically **P**oor **P**erformance!

## What to take with you

This of course will depend on whether you are competing near home or travelling abroad. If you are racing abroad you may need to think about taking extra items of clothing for a variety of weather conditions. The New York Marathon,

for instance, is known for completely unpredictable weather conditions – from snow to warm days. Similarly, we have lost count of the number of times athletes' bags have gone missing when travelling, so it makes sense to always take your race kit and race shoes in your hand luggage. If something is going to go wrong, by either getting lost, stolen or broken, then you want to have spares ready to hand rather than have to go rushing around an un-familiar town looking for a running shop to replace the vital piece of kit the day before the race.

### Packing

A week before you go – especially if you are going abroad – it's best to have a 'dry run' to make sure you have everything you need and that you have room to carry it all. Start by

# WHAT TO TAKE WITH YOU: CHECKLIST

## Clothing

- Racing vest and shorts (take enough training kit to cover any training sessions you may do in your final approach to the race day)
- Socks
- For a major event, consider wearing old clothes and/or a bin liner to the start line, which you can throw away, as you may need to place bags on baggage buses a considerable amount of time before the start
- Racing shoes and training shoes
- Rain jacket
- Spare long- and short-sleeved T-shirts
- Running tights, tracksuit and spare clothes for post-race
- Hat (summer and winter)
- Running gloves
- Pins
- Comfy shoes/flip-flops for post-race
- Compression tights.

## Other kit and energy products

- Extra bag for race day
- Water bottles
- Bottle brush
- Detergent for cleaning bottles
- Washing powder for clothing
- Energy gels
- Energy drinks (in powder form)
- Pre- and post-race snacks and breakfast
- Plasters and Vaseline for the bits that get rubbed
- Sun cream (and possibly after-sun moisturiser)
- First-aid kit
- Book, music player, electronic games for relaxation for the pre-race day (to help you relieve boredom and stay off your feet).

getting together everything on our checklist, above.

Then get your suitcase and try packing it. All those running shoes take up a considerable amount of space and, once these have been packed, you may not have a lot of space for other things you may want to take. A good tip is to put a holdall in there with clothing to save having to carry another bag.

If you are travelling by air it's a good idea to weigh the whole thing before you go, to make sure you don't fall foul of excess-baggage charges.

## The day before

If you are travelling abroad to race you will probably arrive at least one day before the event, but preferably two or three days before. For large, city marathons you will usually use this day to get to the race expo, and pick up your race number and transponder (the electronic device worn on your shoe to allow for automatic tracking of your progress during the race).

On the day before the race, you may want to do a bit of sight-seeing, but it's best to put this off until after the event. Resting before race day is vital. Remember: don't stand if you can sit down, and don't sit down if you can lie down! Now is the time for resting and gathering your thoughts.

Remember the rules laid down in chapter 11 about the importance of getting as much

carbohydrate as possible on board in the days leading up to the race. The day before the race is about resting as much as possible and eating as much high-carbohydrate food as you feel comfortable with.

On the day of the race, make sure you have plenty of time to get to the start. If you are reliant on public transport, know the times of your planned method of transport and plan a back-up route in case of delays or cancellations. Ensure you have directions to get you to the start, not just the local area. And, most important of all, make sure you plan your arrival in plenty of time to ensure a toilet stop and an adequate warm-up for your relevant event.

### Know the route and leave yourself a note

Knowing the route you will race in detail is an essential part of your preparation. You should have studied the route many months before, as knowing the challenge you face is an essential prerequisite to structuring your training programme.

This will help you to plan for any difficult points on the course, where there may be tough hills, and where you can benefit from feed stations. This should also be used to help you with pacing. Having split times written on your hand or on a pacing band can be of real value. Knowing your splits at certain points will ensure that you don't get caught up in the spirit of the day, overdo things early on and suffer in the latter stages.

Make use of this information carefully, however. If the weather is warmer than expected, you may need to think on your feet and alter the pacing you had originally hoped for. Similarly, relying on a GPS watch in a big city may be problematic as the signals can be subject to interference with high-rise buildings. Likewise, your heart rate monitor may suffer from cross-talk if there are other people in close proximity wearing the same brand. In all these cases you need to have an alternative back-up plan. Having to make changes to your planned strategy is very difficult when you are fatigued from running at race pace.

## Race-day nutrition strategies

Before the event you need to plan your strategy. If you are staying away from home, what are you going to eat and when? Consider taking your own foods with you, and know how you respond to eating them. Rather than being reliant on the foods provided in a hotel, you will be confident that you can eat what you prefer. Have any energy bars ready, or drinks pre-mixed if you are planning to use these as part of your pre-race build. Use a bottle that you are prepared to leave behind – the less you carry with you, the more energy you are saving for the race effort.

Most running events are extremely well organised and you will find several feeding stations along the route. As well as water, many provide energy drinks, and some even hand out gels en route. That said, if you are familiar with a certain product it may be worth sticking with

**Figure 13.1 The start**

what you know. In this case it may mean using a combination of gels and water, but a well-prepared athlete will know exactly the amount they will need for the weather conditions and pace, as they will be well used to practising that strategy during training.

## Race tactics

After completing your training you may be good enough to go to your targeted event and be in contention for victory. Even if you are not expecting to be near the front, and your only glimpse of the leaders is their backs on the start line, you will still be aiming to get to the finish as quickly as possible. So you may think that race tactics aren't as important to you as they would be to someone aiming to win. That may be so, but it is still worth considering your tactical approach to the race.

Maybe you have set yourself a target of achieving a particular finishing time or race position. Whatever your aim, it will be affected by the other runners around you. When the starting signal sounds, often the red mist comes down and all thoughts leave your mind for a short while; at this point you can get dragged along with the crowd. This is not a good situation.

## Pacing

From the training you have done the best approach to any endurance race is to maintain as even a pace as possible. There's no point in sprinting away from the start line as this will cause you to go into oxygen debt and to fatigue far earlier in the event than necessary. There is, in fact, a wealth of scientific evidence that suggests negative pacing (running the first part of the race slower than the second half) is far more beneficial to overall performance than going off harder and hoping to hang on.

## Training partners

Many of you will have a buddy you have spent many hours training alongside in the build-up to a big event. Finding someone to share those long runs or hard interval sessions with is great for motivation. Often training partners end up targeting the same event and may have a plan to run the event together.

That's fine if you both agree to help each other on the day regardless of the difference in ability. But it is worth being aware that no two athletes will ever perform at the same level. There will always be one that is stronger than the other, and you need to be aware of this. It is not unusual to go through highs and lows during a long-distance event, and these are unlikely to happen at the same time for both athletes. While your buddy may be there to help you through and give you the motivation you need, having to slow for you may ruin their chance of the race of their life.

If you want to run the whole distance with someone, you have to agree the rules beforehand. You have to accept that the stronger athlete is going to have to slow down to allow the weaker runner to keep pace. If you want to go for a time, it's best just to set off at your own pace and meet up after the finish. Some runners start marathons with a friend, lose contact with each other in the crowds during the opening kilometres and don't see each other again until the finish – then realise that they crossed the line less than a minute apart! It's a good idea to have a plan about where to meet after the race and to have a back-up if 'plan A' fails. Taking your mobile phone with you and putting it in your post-race bag is the best bet, but be aware you may struggle for network coverage with so many other individuals trying to keep in contact with friends and family.

# It's all in the mind . . .

Whether you are an Olympic champion or running your first 10 km race, you will experience pain when running hard. In the marathon this will most likely happen between 18 and 22 miles. Running at pace for any distance is not only a test of physical fitness, it is also a test of mental strength. At the elite level, athletes are often closely matched physically; what determines who wins on a given day will be who is the best tactically, but also who can push themselves the hardest when the going gets tough.

If you are going to produce the best performance you are capable of, then you have to have a plan for dealing with those moments when the pain and suffering you experience make you feel like giving up. Some runners are naturally more determined than others, but we can all learn some techniques that will help us get through those tough times.

## Association and disassociation

These are two ways of dealing with the pain of running when you are at your physical limits. If you are suffering, and your legs are starting to become heavy and sluggish, or even cramp, and you decide to get through it by concentrating more on your running technique or by concentrating on your breathing, that's associating with the pain. You are focusing on factors that affect your performance and that can have an effect on your pace. Ideally, you want to think about being relaxed, losing stress and tension, and feeling light or 'driving' your arms.

Disassociation is looking for something to concentrate on that is external to the feelings you are experiencing. For example, you may wish to count the white lines on the road as they pass under your feet, or focus on the back of the runner in front of you, and try to keep them at the same distance or even get closer to them. No one method is better than another – it's just a question of which one works best for the individual.

## Thinking ahead

There are also techniques that you can learn before you get to race day. One can help in training and racing, and involves spending a little time practising a positive thinking routine. You need to do this when you have some time to relax and lie down alone with your thoughts. Some music may help. Think of a session where you felt really strong, fit and full of energy. Remember how it felt when you ran relaxed, driving and flowing, the feeling you had in your legs, and how easy it was to push off the pavement, lift your knees and move forward. The point of this is to tap into this feeling of being strong and confident when you experience moments when you feel tired and weak.

You need a trigger to remind you that you are strong and can overcome moments of weakness. The trigger can be the music you play when focusing on positive thinking. In a race, recalling the music, or even humming it, can help you focus on being positive and pushing through the pain.

177

**Figure 13.2 The aftermath**

even an ice bath. But, after a big event, that ideal world may be a million miles away. Often with a large number of entrants you won't easily be able to get to your pre-prepared recovery drink – you may be looking for friends that you did the event with, or relatives who have come to support you. The best advice here is to get whatever you can to eat and drink. Soak up the atmosphere and share your experiences with those around you. Recovery may take a few days longer than is ideal, but with

Alternatively, you can get a brightly coloured square of paper and focus on that colour during your positive thinking session. When you have a race coming up, you can get a coloured square of paper and stick it on your race watch. When the going gets tough you can glance at the coloured square to tap into that feeling of strength and confidence when you need it most. It may sound unconventional, but it can work.

## It's all over: how to recover

Never again! That's the first thought of many as they cross the finish line in a mixture of agony and ecstasy. That thought may stay with you for a few days as your legs and body slowly start to recover from the effort you have put in. But there will still be elation – you did it!

In an ideal world you should now be following many of the strategies outlined earlier in the book: consume a recovery drink; have a light jog to clear your legs; drink plenty of fluids to rehydrate; have a stretch or a massage, maybe

**Figure 13.3 Don't underestimate the importance of post-exercise recovery**

the big day over you need to give yourself a recovery week . . . or two!

In the first few hours after the event, continue to eat and drink as much as you comfortably can. Try to keep moving, to keep your body loose, and think about your journey home. If you are leaving the next day, you may not feel like it, but it may be sensible to pack your bags with as much of your kit as you physically can (leaving it to the next day when you are stiff and sore makes the job even harder). After that, go and soak up the atmosphere of the event with your fellow competitors. Share stories, relive your experiences and soak up the camaraderie. You may still be thinking 'never again', but it will make the event even more memorable.

Once back home, one of the first things many do is look on the internet for their results. This is where the motivation often starts to reappear. An analysis of results, for overall, gender or age placing, and an analysis of your race day, will often give an idea of where lessons can be learned, time gained or strategies improved to see an overall improvement in results. This is often when many start planning for the next 'big one', be it a repeat of the same event next year, a move to a different distance or even an attempt at something new, like a triathlon.

Whatever the choice, go back to basics: make a note of what worked for you, where improvements could have been made in training, nutrition or on race day, and start planning for your next big day . . .

Good luck!

# USEFUL WEBSITES

**100 Marathon Club** (a club for those who have completed 100 marathons, but also great for its links): www.100marathonclub.org.uk

**Canadian Society for Exercise Physiology** (a copy of the Physical Activity Readiness Questionnaire (PAR-Q) can be found here): http://www.csep.ca/communities/c574/files/hidden/pdfs/par-q.pdf

**English Institute of Sport**: www.eis2win.co.uk

**ExRx.net** (Exercise Prescription on the Net – a free resource for the exercise professional, coach or fitness enthusiast): www.exrx.net

**Fell Runners Association of Great Britain**: www.fell-runner.org.uk

**Fit Day** (free diet and weight loss journal; if you need to analyse your dietary intake or energy expenditure, you can self-log this information here; the site allows you to track your food, exercise, weight loss and nutritional goals): www.fitday.com

**Functional Movement Screen** (FMS): www.functional-movement.com

**Garmin** (with a wide range of GPS systems designed specifically for athletes, enabling you to track your pace and speed, as well as where you have been, and plot new routes): www.garmin.com

**London Marathon** (official site of the ever-popular London Marathon, with race entries and information): www.london-marathon.co.uk

**Map My Run** (if you don't own a GPS and want to work out how far you are running, or you want to plot the distance of a new route, then this site has mapping software that allows you to track a route and its profile): www.mapmyrun.com

**National Strength & Conditioning Association** (the worldwide authority on strength and conditioning): www.nsca-lift.org

**Perform: Fitness:** (Alex Reid's strength and conditioning company): www.performfitness.co.uk

**Polar heart rate monitors** (world-leading heart rate monitor manufacturer): www.polar.fi

**Runner's World** (websites of the popular magazine *Runner's World*; lots of up-to-date information and articles, with very active forums; easily searchable race diaries): www.runnersworld.com, www.runnersworld.co.uk

**Running for Fitness** (a very useful resource site, with race pace calculators and various other predictors): www.runningforfitness.org

**Science in Sport** (leading sports nutrition company): www.scienceinsport.com

**Sports Injury Clinic** (virtual sports injury site and injury advice): www.sportsinjuryclinic.net

**Sports Medicine** (information about sports medicine and workouts for athletes): www.sportsmedicine.about.com

**Sportscience** (a journal and site for sport research): www.sportsci.org

**Sportstest Ltd** (Dr Garry Palmer's sports physiology company): www.sportstest.co.uk

**UK Athletics** (governing body for UK athletics – track and field – with events, results, features and profiles): www.ukathletics.net

**UK Results.net** (UK-based race information and results service; events are archived as far back as 1979, but extensive from 1993): www.UKResults.net

**UK Sport** (the UK's high-performance sports agency): www.uksport.gov.uk

**UltraRunner** (the US site for ultra running events): www.ultrarunner.com

**United Kingdom Strength and Conditioning Association** (the professional body for strength and conditioning in the UK): www.uksca.org.uk

**World Marathon Majors** (if you fancy a marathon further afield, Boston, Berlin, Chicago and New York are all served by this site): www.worldmarathonmajors.com

**Zone Five Software** (the site of SportTracks, an exercise logbook software, which you can use to store, log and analyse GPS, heart rate and other training data from a wealth of different devices): www.zonefivesoftware.com

# REFERENCES

Armstrong, L.E. (2000) *Performing in Extreme Environments*, Champaign, IL: Human Kinetics.

Bergstrom, J., Hermansen, L., Hultman, E. and Saltin, B. (1967), Diet, muscle glycogen and physical performance, *Acta Physiologica Scandinavica*, 71, 140–150.

Berry, M.J. and McMurray, R.G. (1987), Effects of graduated compression stockings on blood lactate following an exhaustive bout of exercise, *American Journal of Physical Medicine*, 66, 121–132.

Blair, S., Ellsworth, M., Haskell, W., Stern, M., Farquhar, J. & Wood, P. (1981), Comparison of nutrient intake in middle-aged men and women runners and controls, *Medicine and Science in Sports and Exercise*, 13, 310–315.

Bompa, T.O. (1999), *Periodisation. Theory and Methodology of Training* (4th edn), Champaign, IL: Human Kinetics.

Borg, G. (1998), *Borg's Rating of Perceived Exertion and Pain Scales,* Champaign, IL: Human Kinetics.

Brouns, F. (1991), Heat, sweat, dehydration, rehydration: a praxis oriented approach, *Journal of Sports Sciences*, 9, Special Issue, 143–152.

Bruckner, P. and Khan, K. (2001), *Clinical Sports Medicine* (2nd edn), Australia: McGraw-Hill Book Company.

Buist, I., Bredeweg, S.W., Bassem, B., Van Mechelen, W., Lemmink, K.A. and Diercks, R.L. (2008), Incidence and risk factors of running related injuries during preparation for a four-mile recreational running event, *British Journal of Sports Medicine*, 16 May.

Buist, I., Bredeweg, S.W., Lemmink, K.A., Pepping, G.J., Zwerver, J., Van Mechelen, W. and Diercks, R.L. (2007), The GRONORUN study: is a graded training program for novice runners effective in preventing running related injuries? Design of a randomized controlled trial, *British Medical Council (BMC) Musculoskeletal Disorders*, 8, 2 March, 24.

Chartered Society of Physiotherapy (1998), *PRICE Guidelines: guidelines for the management of soft tissue (musculoskeletal) injury with Protection, Rest Ice, Compression and Elevation (PRICE) during the first 72 hours (ACPSM),* Chartered Society of Physiotherapy.

Cinque, C. (1989), Massage for cyclists: the winning touch? *The Physician and Sports Medicine*, 17(10), 167–170.

Clanton, T.O. and Coupe, K.J. (1998), Hamstring strains in athletes: diagnosis and treatment, *Journal of the American Academy of Orthopaedic Surgeons*, 6(4), Jul–Aug, 237–248.

Costill, D.L. and Miller, J.M. (1980), Nutrition for endurance sport: carbohydrate and fluid balance. *International Journal of Sports Medicine*, 1, 2–14.

Coyle, E. (1995), Integration of the physiological factors determining endurance performance ability, *Exercise and Sport Sciences Reviews*, 23, 25–63.

Daniels, J. and Gilbert, J. (1979), *Oxygen Power: Performance Tables for Distance Runners,* Daniels and Gilbert.

Foster, C. and Lucia, A. (2007), Running economy, *Sports Medicine*, 37(4/5), 316.

Fredericson, M. and Moore, T. (2005), Core stabilisation training for middle and long-distance runners, *Physical Medicine and Rehabilitation Clinics of North America*, 16(3), August, 669–689.

Fry, R.W., Morton, A.R. and Keast, D. (1991), Overtraining in athletes. An update, *Sports Medicine (Auckland, NZ)*, 12(1), Jul, 32–65.

Gambetta, V. (2007), *Athletic Development: The Art and Science of Functional Sports Conditioning.* Champaign, IL: Human Kinetics

Gill, N.D., Beaven, C.M. and Cook, C. (2006), Effectiveness of post-match recovery strategies in rugby players, *British Journal of Sports Medicine*, 40, 260–263.

Hodges, P.W. and Richardson, C.A. (1996), Inefficient muscular stabilization of the lumbar spine associated with low back pain: a motor control evaluation of transversus abdominis, Spine, 21(22), 15 November, 2640–2650.

Hubbard, T.J. and Hicks-Little, C.A. (2008), Ankle ligament healing after an acute ankle sprain: an evidence-based approach, *Journal of Athletic Training*, 43(5), Sep-Oct, 523–529.

International Olympic Committee (2003) IOC Consensus Statement on Sports Nutrition. Available at: http://www.olympic.org/uk/utilities/reports/level2_uk.asp?HEAD2=1&HEAD1=1.

Johnston, R.E. MS, Quinn, T.J. PhD, Kertzer, R. PhD,

Vroman, N.B. PhD (1995), Improving running economy through strength training, *Strength & Conditioning*, 17(4), August, 7–13.

Knobloch, K., Yoon, U. and Vogt, P.M. (2008), Acute and over-use injuries correlated to hours of training in master running athletes, *Foot and Ankle International Journal*, 29(7), Jul, 671–676.

Macera, C.A. (1992), Lower extremity injuries in runners, advances in prediction. *Sports Medicine New Zealand*, 13(1), Jan, 50–57.

Martin, B.J. (1981), Effects of sleep deprivation on tolerance of prolonged exercise, *European Journal of Applied Physiology and Occupational Physiology*, 47, 345–354.

Morgan, W. and Borg, G.A. (1976), Perception of effort in the prescription of physical activity. In Nelson, T. (ed.), *Mental Health and Emotional Aspects of Sports*. Chicago: American Medical Association, 126–129.

Moritani, T. and Devries, H.A. (1979), Neural factors versus hypertrophy in the time course of muscle strength gain, *American Journal of Physical Medicine*, 58, 115–130.

National Strength and Conditioning Association (1993), Position statement: Explosive/plyometric exercise, *NSCA Journal*, 15(3), 16.

Nieman, D.C. and Pederson, B.K. (1999), *Exercise and Immune Function. Recent Developments,* Department of Health and Exercise Science, Appalachian State University, Boone, North Carolina.

Nieman, D.C. (1997), Risk of upper respiratory tract infection in athletes: an epidemiologic and immunologic perspective, *Journal of Athletic Training*, 32(4), Oct, 344–349.

Nobel, B.J., Borg, G.A., Jacobs, I. *et al.* (1983), A category-ratio perceived exertion scale: relationship to blood and muscle lactates and heart rate, *Medicine and Science in Sports and Exercise*, 15, 523–528.

Palmer, G.S., Borghouts, L.B., Noakes, T.D. and Hawley, J.A. (1999), Metabolic and performance responses to constant-load vs variable-intensity exercise in trained cyclists, *Journal of Applied Physiology*, 87(3), September, 1186–1196.

Prentice, W. (1990), *Therapeutic Modalities in Sports Medicine* (2nd edn), St Louis: Times Mirror/Mosby College.

Robergs, R.A. and Roberts. S. (1997), *Exercise Physiology: Exercise, Performance, and Clinical Applications,* Mosby.

Saltin, B. and Costill, D.L. (1988), Fluid and electrolyte balance during prolonged exercise. In E.S. Horton and R.L. Terjung (eds), *Exercise, Nutrition and Energy Metabolism,* New York: Macmillan.

Saunders, P.U., Pyne, D.B., Telford, R.D. and Hawley, J.A. (2004), Factors affecting running economy in trained distance runners, *Sports Medicine*, 34(7), 465–485.

Sjodin, B. and Svedenhag, J. (1985), Applied physiology of marathon running, *Sports Medicine*, 2, 83–99.

Spurrs, R.W., Murphy, A.J. and Watsford, M.L. (2003), The effect of plyometric training on distance running performance, *European Journal of Applied Physiology*, 89(1), Mar, 1–7 (e-published 24 December 2002).

Taunton, J.E., Ryan, M.B., Clement, D.B., McKenzie, D.C., Lloyd-Smith, D.R. and Zumbo, B.D. (2002), A retrospective case-control analysis of 2002 running injuries, *British Journal of Sports Medicine*, 36(2), April, 95–101.

Trenell, M.I., Rooney, K.B., Sue, C.M. and Thompson, C.H. (2006), Compression garments and recovery from eccentric exercise: a 31P-Mrs study, *Journal of Sports Science and Medicine*, 5, 106–114.

Uusitalo, A.L.T., Tahvanainen, K.U.O., Uusitalo, A.J. and Rusko, H.K. (1996), Does increase in training intensity vs volume influence supine and standing heart rate and heart rate variability? Over-training and Over-reaching in Sport Congress, Memphis, Tennessee.

Walters, P.H. (2002), Sleep, the athlete and performance, *Strength & Conditioning*, 24(2), 17–24.

Wilmore, J.H. & Costill, D. (1994), *Physiology of Sport and Exercise,* Champaign, IL: Human Kinetics.

Wisløff, U., Castagna, C., Helgerud, J., Jones, R. and Hoff, J. (2004), Strong correlation of maximal squat strength with sprint performance and vertical jump height in elite soccer players, *British Journal of Sports Medicine*, 38, 285–288.

Yamaguchi, T., Ishii, K., Yamanaka, M. and Yasuda, K. (2006), Acute effect of static stretching on power output during concentric dynamic constant external resistance leg extension, *Journal of Strength and Conditioning Research*, 20(4), Nov, 804–810.

# INDEX

**a**
Achilles tendinopathy 64–6
ankle sprain 82–7

**b**
baths 98–9
blisters 73

**c**
carbohydrates 133, 139, 141–3
  and racing 155–7
  and recovery 146
  and training 148–53
  and weight loss 166–7
circulation 9–11, 42
  see also heart rate
compression garments 100–1
concentric load 81
core function 88–91

**d**
developmental flexibility 43
DOMS (delayed onset muscle soreness) 94
dynamic flexibility 44–5

**e**
eccentric load 81–2
endurance (END) training 36, 111
endurance performance model 13–14
energy:
  balance 168–9
  nutritional requirements for 164–6
  production 11–12

**f**
fat (body) 139–40, 160–2
fat (dietary) 133, 134
feet 71–5
  see also shoes
field testing for fitness 29–32
fitness testing 33–5
  field testing 29–32
  self-administered treadmill test 28–9
FIT principle 51
five keys for training 22–3

flexibility and stretching 42–9
Formula One car comparison 20–1, 132
functional drills 104–19
functional movement patterns 45
fungal infections 74

**g**
gels 152, 173
goal-setting 17–18

**h**
hamstring injury 78–81
heart rate 26–7, 52
  field testing 29–32
  and over-training 56–8
  resting 57
  self-administered treadmill testing 28–9
  training zones 35–9
  see also circulation
heat 76–8
hill running 117–19
hydration 136–7, 143–4, 158
  and recovery 93–4, 146–8
  and training 153–4
hypertrophy 111

**i**
ice 75, 76–8, 98–9
iliotibial band friction syndrome (ITB) 65, 70
illness 16, 26, 50, 52, 53–4
injury 50, 64–70, 72, 86–8
  feet 73–4
  and stretching 42
  and training 16
  see also ankle sprain; hamstring injury

**k**
knee injury 64, 65, 67

**m**
massage 97–8
mixed muscle zone (MMZ) 36–7
monitors for heart rate 26–7
muscle memory 105
myofascial release 46–7

**n**

needs analysis 18–20
nutrition 132–8
  and energy balance 168–9
  and energy requirements 164–6
  and physical activity 139–44
  and races 155–8, 175
  and recovery 93, 145–8
  and training 148–55
nutritional supplements 52, 53

**o**

overload principle 23–4
over-training 26, 52–62
oxygen 8–9, 10, 12–13, 139–40

**p**

PAR-Q (physical activity readiness questionnaire) 27, 63
performance velocity 13–14
periodisation 24–6
physiology 8–15
plantar fasciitis 64–5, 68–70
plyometrics 115–17
PNF (proprioceptive neuromuscular facilitation) technique 45–6
PRICE principle 75–6, 78
programme design 120–9
progressive overload 25–6, 72
proprioception 84–5
protein 133–5, 143, 146
psychology 94–5, 177–8
pyramids:
  food 138
  training 24–6

**r**

races:
  choosing 17, 20–1
  and nutrition 155–8, 175
  psychology 177–8
  tactics for 175–6
  travel to 172–4
range of movement (ROM) 43, 47–8
rating of perceived exertion (RPE) scale 51–2
recovery 23, 54, 96–101
  after races 178–9
  and nutrition 145–8
  techniques for 92–5
recovery/base (R&B) training 35–6

resisted training 117–18
rest 58, 95–6, 96
  and diet 137–8
  and strength training 108
resting heart rate (RHR) 57–8, 60
risks of exercising 27–8
running drills, speed and agility 104–7
running economy 15, 111–12

**s**

screening 63–4
self-administered treadmill fitness test 28–9
shin splints 64–5, 67–8
shoes 19, 20, 71–2
sleep 96–7
specificity 22–3
speed and power (S&P) training 37–8
static stretching 43
strength training 107–14, 111
stretching and flexibility 42–9, 97
supercompensation 92–3
systems of the body 13

**t**

tactics for races 175–6
testing 28–35
tibial stress syndrome 64–5, 67–8
training 16–21
  FIT principle 51
  five key elements 22–3
  and nutrition 148–55
  physiological testing 28–35
  running drills, speed and agility 104–7
  strength 107–14, 111
  zones 35–9
  *see also* heart rate; PAR-Q
training camps 154–5
training partners 176
travelling to events 157–8, 172–5

**u**

upper respiratory tract infections (URTIs) 52, 53–4

**w**

water *see* hydration
weight loss 166–7

**z**

zones, training 35–9